Christ Changing Lives

Changed Lives Changing Lives

Series Preface

The "Changed Lives Changing Lives" series contains three books that cover the ministry of Christian "disciple investing." As a series, the books address the following aspects of pouring into followers and disciples of Jesus: methodology (*The "Disciple Investing" Life*), philosophy (*Christ Changing Lives*) and relational modeling (*The "Disciple Investing" Apostle*). Whether you are a novice in ministering to others, a seasoned veteran in Christian education, or looking for some inspiration to gain motivation for sharing your life on behalf of others, the "Changed Lives Changing Lives" series is here to help. The author's hope is that the reader will benefit from each book in the series, and that the kingdom of Christ will benefit from the fruit of the changed lives of impacted "disciple investors."

Christ Changing Lives

Digging Deeper into the Practice of Disciple Investing

Rod Culbertson

WIPF & STOCK · Eugene, Oregon

CHRIST CHANGING LIVES
Digging Deeper into the Practice of Disciple Investing

Changed Lives Changing Lives Series 1

Copyright © 2018 Rod Culbertson. All rights reserved. Except for brief quotations in critical publications or reviews, no part of this book may be reproduced in any manner without prior written permission from the publisher. Write: Permissions, Wipf and Stock Publishers, 199 W. 8th Ave., Suite 3, Eugene, OR 97401.

Wipf & Stock
An Imprint of Wipf and Stock Publishers
199 W. 8th Ave., Suite 3
Eugene, OR 97401

www.wipfandstock.com

PAPERBACK ISBN: 978-1-5326-3362-1
HARDCOVER ISBN: 978-1-5326-3364-5
EBOOK ISBN: 978-1-5326-3363-8

Unless otherwise indicated, all Scripture quotations are from The Holy Bible, English Standard Version® (ESV®), copyright © 2001 by Crossway, a publishing ministry of Good News Publishers. Used by permission. All rights reserved.

Manufactured in the U.S.A.

With much gratitude for the sovereign hand of the Lord in my life while a student at the University of South Carolina, I dedicate this book to my former USC roommate, McVey Graham, Jr. ("Mack") and his wife, Doris, both of whom believe that Christ changes lives. The Lord was pleased to allow me to watch the Holy Spirit bring Mack into God's kingdom in our dorm room one fall afternoon in 1973, an act that took place right before my very eyes. I am eternally grateful that I am able to retain this experience as a vivid memory in my mind and heart. It was one of the greatest acts of the Holy Spirit that I have ever experienced! Through the ministry of Wycliffe Bible Translators, Mack and Doris have served Jesus Christ and his church for almost 34 years in an obscure but gospel needy region based in the mountains of Papua New Guinea. May Christ continue to use their translation work to change lives and expand his kingdom!

Contents

Acknowledgments | ix
My (Brief) Personal Story | xi
Introduction | xv

1 Definitions | 1
2 Recognizing a Disciple | 11
3 Paul's Perspective on Disciple Investing | 17
4 The Process: Influences in Disciple Investing | 22
5 Disciple Investing Encounters | 33
6 Spiritual Diagnosis | 43
7 Methods and Models of Discipleship | 59
8 Balanced Disciple Investing | 81
9 Working it Out in Ministry | 98
　Conclusion: Christ is Still Changing Lives | 127

Bibliography | 137

Illustrations

Figure 1: The Prototype Model | 86
Figure 2: The Truth Model | 88
Figure 3: The Righteousness Model | 90
Figure 4: The Love Model | 92
Figure 5: The High Demand Model | 94
Figure 6: The Impossible Model | 95
Figure 7: The Healthy Model | 97

Acknowledgments

A SPECIAL WORD OF thanks must be given to my RTS Charlotte teaching assistant, Ms. Anna Unkefer, who spent countless hours editing this work and refining it for publication. She is an invaluable asset in my efforts toward publishing the books I have written. Also, I must thank one diligent reader of this work, who most certainly helped to improve it with her observations, Mrs. Karen Chacko, who provided many fine contributions to an almost finished product. Both of these very capable ladies' assistance is deeply appreciated by the author.

My (Brief) Personal Story

I HAVE ALWAYS BEEN a part of the local church. Raised in a conservative, fundamental Southern Baptist culture for the first seventeen years of my life, I observed and learned much about the Christian life. Whether I was a Christian during those years is a question that is difficult for me to answer. But I am convinced of one undeniable reality: as a child growing up, the church discipled me through almost every activity; and there were plenty of opportunities. I attended Sunday School, Sunday morning worship, Sunday evening Training Union (Christian Education), Sunday evening worship, mid-week Royal Ambassadors (Southern Baptist boys' program), Vacation Bible School, multiple week-long revival meetings, gatherings sponsored by men in the church, and extra-curricular sports. My mother, who took me to all of these, was wholeheartedly committed to everything the church did. I was present whenever the church doors were open—without exception (faking illness was not an option). The only activity I never participated in was the church camp program; I was shy and didn't want to spend the night in strange places (plus I hate camping and flunked out of Cub Scouts in the second grade!)

In reality, I was saturated with (or immersed in) the teachings of Scripture and Southern Baptist doctrine. My teachers, mother's friends, and my coaches loved me, though frankly, I mostly didn't notice or care. Yet I am convinced that the vestiges of my training still remain rooted in the strict lifestyle of Southern Baptist behavior. I heard truth, saw love (although I didn't recognize, receive, or apply it), and lived out external righteousness with a passion for conformity to God's law and acceptance by whomever was watching. Although I had been discipled, I was not a true disciple of Jesus Christ.

MY (BRIEF) PERSONAL STORY

When I attended college at age seventeen at the University of South Carolina, a hundred miles from home, I was sure I would leave God and my religious upbringing behind. But I could not run from God. My rigid training prevented me from skipping church, even on my very first Sunday away from home; the guilt was too great. But God used that guilt to reach my deep, heartfelt needs, and I surrendered my life to Christ (reluctantly, I might add). Having been raised in the church, I was discipled as what I would term a (non-baptized) covenant child. But being now converted, I became a true follower of Jesus Christ. I joined First Baptist Church of Columbia, South Carolina, another Southern Baptist church, affectionately known as "The Fellowship of Excitement." I also got plugged in with two parachurch campus ministries while in college, the Navigators and Campus Crusade for Christ (now known as Cru). God worked in me, changing every facet of my life. The Navigators stressed biblical knowledge and Scripture memory. Cru spoke incessantly of the love of God (a theme which was contagious), the need for constant evangelism and outreach, and reliance upon the Holy Spirit in the Christian life. First Baptist was biblically based like my home church, but there was an atmosphere filled with the life of the Spirit that I had never experienced before. God sent people into my life who taught, demonstrated, and modeled the life of Jesus Christ. I cannot list them all and can't even remember all of their names, but this I know: I was finally alive! I could not imagine anything more meaningful than being a disciple of Jesus.

Eventually, I became a student leader in Cru and was involved in discipleship relationships with a number of students and non-students. Through the years, both friends in Inter-Varsity Christian Fellowship and IVP authors, as well as Columbia Bible College (now Columbia International University) influenced me. I attended First Baptist Church of Taylors, South Carolina where I was able to serve the church and even disciple others, particularly during the summer months. Eventually, I left my Baptist circles for Bible churches, and in time, I became a convinced Presbyterian. Churches which made a huge impact on my spiritual development after college, and to whom I am indebted for all sorts of learning and growth, are: Eastside Presbyterian in Greenville, South Carolina; Covenant Presbyterian in Columbia, South Carolina; Faith Presbyterian in Gainesville, Florida; Christ Community Presbyterian in Clearwater, Florida; Stonebridge Presbyterian Church and Christ the King Presbyterian Mission (now closed), both in Charlotte, North Carolina.

MY (BRIEF) PERSONAL STORY

Over the years, I have been discipled by pastors, friends, peers, Scripture, prayer meetings, evangelism training and opportunities, Sunday school teachers, church deacons, university and seminary professors, conference and seminar speakers, pamphlets and books, radio and television ministers, various film and video series, Christian musicians, choral events, Christian service opportunities, and a host of others. The Holy Spirit was in charge of the entire process because he is truly the one who orchestrates the discipleship process.

Discipleship is following Jesus. Discipleship is a process which involves a full-orbed, multi-dimensional impact by the Holy Spirit in the life of the follower of Jesus Christ. Discipleship is simply God changing us through the process of gradual and progressive sanctification (growth in Christlikeness). He uses the means of grace, applied in various fashions. He also uses people, his servants, to assist in the change he desires, and all of this is done sovereignly through his Holy Spirit. And, as we all have experienced, he works in his providence, on his designated timetable for our lives.

Introduction

UNDER THE INSPIRATION OF the Holy Spirit, Luke, the author of Acts, perceptively enjoins the reader in the unfolding drama of the growth of the early church. Portraying Christ's final words prior to his ascension, Luke presents the outline of the book, and records his version of Jesus's Great Commission, "But you will receive power when the Holy Spirit has come upon you, and you will be my witnesses in Jerusalem and in all Judea and Samaria, and to the end of the earth." The impact of this resurrection reunion scene, in which Christ gives his disciples their "marching" orders, along with the assurance that they will be able to obey (the subsequent falling of the Holy Spirit at Pentecost, as promised by Jesus, provided the power and the impetus for the message of the gospel to go forth with great effect), is overwhelming. The book of Acts is indeed a book recording the "acts of the Holy Spirit through the apostles." The original reader, excellent Theophilus ("Lover of God"), as well as the contemporary reader, are both able to join an exciting narrative of gospel declaration, with its many twists and turns of events, leading the first-time reader into much astonishment and curiosity as the drama unfolds. The Holy Spirit indeed builds the church of Jesus Christ and the Kingdom of God through the instruments of God's own choosing: human hands (with a few miracles thrown in for attestation that this is the living God's work!)

The focus of the book of Acts is evangelism, the unapologetic declaration of the good news ("gospel") of Christ's resurrection and God's forgiveness of needy sinners. The narrative of gospel encounter, proclamation, ensuing persecution, and consequential church expansion is a clear thrust of the book. But the Great Commission is not simply about evangelism (proclamation). Rather, it includes, in Jesus's own words, the making of disciples, i.e., the development of true, committed, and dedicated followers of Jesus. The persistence of believers amidst their persecution (a characteristic that the reader observes in the book of Acts), gives credence to the transformational nature of the gospel message. The book of Acts convinces one that in spite of rejections of the message, alongside ministry struggles and opposition, the gospel message produces disciples. The aim of this work is to consider the "process" of making disciples, or true followers of the living and risen Lord Jesus Christ. Some call this process "discipleship." Others call it "disciple making" or "disciple building." I prefer to call the process of helping others become like Jesus "disciple investing."

Disciple Investing: Christ Changing Lives

Why "disciple investing?" I believe that, just as Jesus called his original disciples to follow him, so he still calls millions of disciples to follow him today. Ultimately, Jesus disciples all who respond to his sovereign call in their lives. When one individual pours his life into another individual or group, those recipients grow closer to Jesus and reflect something of his character. That person points others, in word, life, and attitude, to the source: Jesus. That person simply becomes involved in the process of *investing* in the Christian growth of others. Essentially, the investor leads others in such a way that those in whom he invests are changed by Jesus Christ himself. Christ calls, disciples respond, and Christ changes their lives. Disciple investing is all about Jesus: he does the work. We are only investors who point others to him. Everything in the disciple investing process is about him. Dietrich Bonhoeffer once stated, "Christianity without discipleship is always Christianity without Christ."[1] Disciple investing means leading people to the fountain of life and that fountain is Christ.

The Need

However, many will raise the question, "Are those who profess faith in Christ actually willing to respond to another person who wishes to invest in their Christian growth?" In one of his many surveys, George Barna asked this penetrating question: "Would church people entertain the idea of being mentored by someone they trust for the purposes of spiritual

---

1. Bonhoeffer, *The Cost of Discipleship*, 59.

development?" The answer can be found in Barna's book, *Growing True Disciples*,

> Yes. Three-quarters of the born again adults said that if they had that opportunity it would be very valuable. Two-thirds claimed it would be exciting. Half of the believers said it would be an answer to prayer. Intriguingly, half also said being mentored spiritually would be a risk, but one worth taking. Small numbers of believers said such an activity would be too time-consuming (26%), not worth the effort (18%), uncomfortable (17%), and threatening (6%).[2]

Apparently, 50 percent of those believers who responded to Barna's survey said that they had been praying for someone to "invest" in their spiritual growth as a Christian. The thought of this reality both staggers and moves me, as it should any Christian leader, pastor, or serious layperson. Christians want to grow in their walks with Christ and become more like him. Who is there to help? Dr. Howard Hendricks, quoting a forlorn believer in his book, *As Iron Sharpens Iron*, writes that there is a "growing number of [people] who say (usually with great regret), 'I've never had any mentors. I can't recall anyone who took much interest in my development.'"[3] This statement of need and regret surely must press the desire to help upon our souls. "Weak" Christianity seems to surround us.

The late Dr. Robert Webber observed the following about "churched" Christians. He states, "In a published document entitled 'The International Consultation on Discipleship,' the authors acknowledged:

- 'Many converts to Christianity throughout the world fall away from faith.' [Note: interpret that through your theological grid as you think appropriate.]
- The church is 'marked by a paradox of growth without depth.'
- 'Many living within the church are not living lives of biblical purity, integrity and holiness.'"[4]

One can debate the theology of these statements and the reasoning behind them, but it is easy to observe this tragic reality in the life of all but the most strident of American churches. And one might suggest (or easily conclude) that the failure "in the pews" stems from the church's failure in leadership.

---

2. Barna, *Growing True Disciples*, 53-54.
3. Hendricks, *As Iron Sharpens Iron*, 18.
4. Webber, *Ancient-Future Evangelism*, 13.

INTRODUCTION

Leadership expert Leighton Ford reinforces this conclusion by stating that in the church "... there is an urgent need for the cultivation of godly and spiritual leadership."[5] Disciple investing is the obvious answer for helping young believers in the faith to grow personally, as well as for building future church leadership. This topic carries great import for the future of the church in America and wherever Christ is known. The church's ability to obey and carry forth Christ's Great Commission is her most crucial responsibility until he comes again to reign in visible glory for all to see and acknowledge. Come quickly, Lord Jesus!

---

5. Ford, *The Making of a Leader*, 10.

1

Definitions

Thinking Through Disciple Investing

The International Consultation on Discipleship

As we think through this process of "Disciple Investing," we will find it helpful to hear from various authors and practitioners. An obvious place to begin would be with the landmark meeting held in 1999 in Eastbourne, England, at the International Consultation on Discipleship. In September of that year, 450 church leaders from fifty four countries and close to ninety Christian denominations and groups met together with a deep concern regarding the body of Christ. This association of key Christian leaders met for the purpose of discussing the frequently observed problem of individuals professing faith in Christ but not actually following Christ as true, committed disciples. At the First International Consultation on Discipleship, the late John R. W. Stott called attention to the "strange and disturbing paradox" of the contemporary Christian situation: we have experienced enormous statistical growth without corresponding growth in discipleship. "God is not pleased," warned Stott, "with superficial discipleship."

Therefore, these leaders from all over the world, representing The International Consultation on Discipleship, proposed a succinct definition for this crucial task of the church:

> "Discipleship is a process that takes place within accountable relationships over a period of time for the purpose of bringing believers to spiritual maturity in Christ. Biblical examples suggest that

discipleship is both relational and intentional, both a position and a process."[1]

Upon reflection, we can learn a few things about discipleship from the above definition:

It is a process. Unlike regeneration (conversion or "being made alive from above"), which is instantaneous (although I would suggest that conversion is also a process), to be a disciple of Jesus involves all of one's life for the duration of one's life. An individual does not become a serious, practicing disciple of Jesus overnight. Because discipleship is a process, it takes time. I would suggest that being a disciple of Jesus is a lifelong endeavor and we are always a work in progress. However, the concept of discipleship includes the commitment to invest in another person's spiritual life for some duration of time. Gathering together and growing together is a priority for those engaged in the process of discipleship.

To be a disciple of Jesus one must think in terms of relationships. Tasks, obedience, ministry, growth in knowledge, and understanding are all part of the process of discipleship, but ultimately the Christian life is relational. The follower of Christ wants to know him, who is eternal life, and to walk with him on a daily basis. We do so aware that we have a destination of seeing him someday face-to-face. Ultimately, we answer to one whom we know personally: the resurrected Christ. The discipleship process reflects these two dimensions: relationships and accountability. Love and responsibility are wedded together. The person being discipled is loved by the discipler. Accountability includes a consistent effort to meet; to be transparent, deal with one's own frailties, weaknesses, and sins; to be encouraged, and to respond to both the relationship and issues discussed together. Both college students and adults can build a relationship of trust, love, and accountability that grows more deeply than the parent-child relationship. This is due to mutual maturity and a sense of sober Christian responsibility. Accountable relationships translate into both impact and change. Christ-likeness, Christ-closeness, and spiritual maturity are the result of this type of dual emphasis, "accountable relationships."

The definition continues, however, to point out one of the great weaknesses of relational ministry. Often, and seemingly inevitably, the nature of relational ministry creates a lack of intentionality in the investment process. There is indeed something powerful about the reality that passion

1. International Consultation, *The Eastbourne Consultation Joint Statement on Discipleship*

is often "caught and not taught" and I do not dismiss this premise in any way. However, although the relationship can spawn all sorts of growth and understanding, one should recognize that the teaching of biblical content, along with specific application and direction, is essential as you work with a person who is willing to be discipled. Meeting together to invest in another person's spiritual growth is not simply for the purpose of building a relationship with that person, but must also include an intentional focus on ministering to the person and addressing specific areas of need in his/her life. There does exist a *position*, i.e., a secure, loving, trusting (and non-overbearing) relationship between the discipler and the disciple (we certainly observe this concept as Jesus works with his disciples). But there is also always a *process* of learning, rebuking, encouraging, and directing the person who is willing to be led in the disciple investing exchange.

Other Definitions

Other definitions of discipleship that might be helpful toward understanding the full scope of this crucial ministry need to be noted:

The Three "I's"

From *The Disciplemaker's Handbook*, Alice Fryling writes that Disciplemaking is "the process of helping someone establish a relationship with Jesus and instructing that friend in the life of faith."[2] She includes three aspects to her definition:

- Disciplemaking is *intentional*.
- Disciplemaking is *individualized*.
- Disciplemaking is *inspired*.[3]

I would like to make just a few observations from Ms. Fryling's definition. First, disciplemaking is *intentional*, i.e., it is not simply organic. People are discipled by Christ in an organic *fashion*; simply by sitting "under" the means of grace (the Word of God, the sacraments and prayer, etc.) these particular means are able to influence their hearts, souls, and lives. However, all those who are involved in ministry recognize that "people run from

2. Fryling, *Disciplemakers' Handbook*, 18.
3. Ibid., 18–19.

God." Therefore, we must seek them and have a vision for them to grow. We go after the straying sheep with the intention of bringing them back to the fold and helping them, as we address their real spiritual needs and the battles that jeopardize their souls.

Secondly, disciplemaking is *individualized*. Disciplemaking is like raising children; you raise each one differently. If you have ever been a parent or if you recall the parenting you received (assuming that you had siblings), you know that each child has different needs, different personalities, different responses, and needs different motivators. This understanding affects the manner in which you relate, teach, correct, and encourage. Disciplemaking is personalized for each individual. I discovered some of the flaws in the disciplemaking process immediately after I became a Christian through the Navigator ministry at the University of South Carolina in 1972. Providentially, I attended the first Navigator Bible study ever held on that campus. I had just become a Christian. The Navigator leadership plan was to use the Navigator published *Design for Discipleship* series material and to begin in book seven, a study in the book of 1 Thessalonians (I still have my copy). Instead of starting a Bible study for new believers (book one), the Navigators decided to focus on a more mature group of Christian students. They didn't exactly follow the Navigator "design for discipleship" prescribed program. Thankfully, having been raised in the church, I was actually well beyond the first few books of the *DFD* curriculum. Had the Navigators followed their (normally) rigid program, I can assure you that I would have dropped out early due to boredom of material. I'm not sure that they personalized their first Bible study with me in mind, but their deviation from a programmatic methodology made the difference in my life.

Finally, Fryling states, "Disciplemaking is *inspired*," i.e., it is a pleasure to invest in another individual's life. Disciplemaking is worth the sacrifices and time invested. I cannot overestimate the pleasure and joy that comes from pouring into another person's life. As difficult and challenging as the process may be, the outcomes are often so rewarding that it is a wonder we don't simply engage in disciple investing for the pleasure and personal reward that seeing someone changed (often right before our eyes) brings to our hearts. This is why the Apostle Paul could write, "For what is our hope or joy or crown of boasting before our Lord Jesus at his coming? Is it not you? For you are our glory and joy" (1 Thess 2:19–20). His enthusiasm for these disciples of Christ abounds!

DEFINITIONS

What are You Producing?

Randy Pope, Pastor of Perimeter Church in Atlanta, and a man seasoned in working with professionals and persons in the world of business, defines discipleship as, "... nothing more than having a life product, being intentional about imparting that product, and spending enough time doing the right things to impart that product."[4] Notice that his definition appears to entail a business type mentality (a *product*) or possibly an approach that reflects the efficiency of a large organization or manufacturer. This definition could sound impersonal. However, from outside observation, I am quite certain that the definition above displays Pastor Pope's determination to be certain that not only will he pour his life into the lives of others, but he also expects his church members to have a similar mentality. If we allowed Pastor Pope to expand this definition, I am confident that he would explain that the "product" is a fully Christ-focused and Christ-centered follower of God. But how does that happen? Conviction, determination, time, and an appraisal by the disciple that she is emphasizing the proper disciplines and topics to ensure (like FDA standards) that those being discipled will have the mind of Christ, as well as hearts and wills for Jesus.

The Key is Transformation

Tom Fillinger is the CEO of IgniteUS, Inc. ministry, a Southern Baptist pastor, and a man on a mission to see transformation in his denomination. He believes that change will come to the local church and to his denomination only if pastors and churches will truly disciple their people. Pastor Fillinger clarifies his view on the necessity of discipleship by stating the following:

> A disciple is a believer who is becoming more like Christ and whose transformation is consistent, objective and measurable.[5]

Transformation comes from the study of Scripture, applying the precepts and principles in daily living, and imitating the life of a disciple as modeled by mature believers. There is deliberate and intentional effort to obey all that Jesus has commanded.

Pastor Fillinger further clarifies, "Transformation is more than information. It must include application. Applied theology is the consistent

---

4. Pope, "Journey Curriculum."
5. Fillinger, "First Person."

integration of truth into daily living. God's truth ultimately shapes every dimension of a disciple's life."[6] Dr. Fillinger believes, as I do, that a true disciple of Jesus is a person who has been changed, is being changed, and will continue to be changed into the likeness of the character of Christ. This change is constant (although steadily intermittent) and comes about through the use, study, and understanding of Scripture. But the Bible is not to be viewed as an avenue of knowledge only. One must apply the truth (theology) to life (practice) every day and in every aspect of one's life. The disciple's life is characterized by comprehensive obedience (whole life) and obedience without compromise (wholehearted). The claims of Jesus are to be taken seriously and responded to with a focused and concerted effort.

An Apprenticeship with Jesus

Eugene Peterson, pastor and author, expresses his succinct definition: "Discipleship (*mathetes*) says we are people who spend our lives apprenticed to our master, Jesus Christ. We are in a growing-learning relationship, always. A disciple is a learner, but not in the academic setting of a schoolroom, rather at the work site of a craftsman. We do not acquire information about God but skills in faith."[7]

Dr. Peterson's explanation affirms the thought that ultimately the believer is being discipled by Jesus, no matter who else might be investing in her life. We learn at Jesus's feet and we grow under his tutelage. But, the lessons involve faith, not simply knowledge and facts. The teacher loves us and leads us all the way in the process of learning to trust him for all of life. I would like to suggest, however, that we do acquire information about God and hopefully a lot of it since he has revealed himself in the Scriptures. But I also agree with Dr. Peterson that we need to both embrace and apply that information so that our lives and faith are enhanced.

On Answering the Call

My good friend Dr. David Sinclair, former RUF Campus Minister at Clemson University and present pastor at Clemson Presbyterian Church writes simply, "A disciple is a *man answering the call of Jesus whose whole*

---

6. Ibid.
7. Peterson, *A Long Obedience in the Same Direction*, 17.

life is redirected in obedience. Discipleship is a lifestyle of wholehearted obedience to Christ."[8] Dr. Sinclair reiterates the emphasis of Pastor Fillinger (above)—his emphasis is on life (or lifestyle), heart, and change. The concept of repentance is included because the direction of the disciple's life has been changed; the person has responded to the person of Jesus and his life has been turned around. Obedience is a key aspect of the true follower of Jesus. In some ways, one might say that obedience is a fruit of any follower of Jesus as Lord.

A New Creature in Christ

Missiologist, author, seminary professor, and church growth specialist Peter Wagner asks the question: "So what is a disciple?" His answer: "A Christian. Disciples are people who have been born again by the Spirit of God . . . Disciples are new creatures in Christ Jesus . . . But in general, the life of a disciple is characterized by continuing 'steadfastly in the apostles' doctrine and fellowship, in the breaking of bread, and in prayers.'"[9]

Dr. Wagner states the most basic of assumptions in a profound way. The disciple of Jesus is a new person, observably new because the individual is born again. The phrase "born again" mystifies the natural man because it speaks of an experience that causes a new heart and creates a new person. This is truly the first step in the change and transformation of the disciple and indicates that a person is truly following Jesus. Such a person has been internally touched by God's Spirit and continues in the faith; this is no temporary life change. Wagner elucidates the character of the Christian disciple by defining the areas of impact upon the born-again believer: teaching, fellowship, sacrament, and prayer.

A Wholehearted Desire to Please God

The mentor who made the biggest impact on my practice of ministry, changing the way I view ministry for life, was Reverend Mr. Mark Lowrey, the founder of Reformed University Ministries, the campus ministry of the Presbyterian Church in America (PCA). Pastor Lowrey states, "A disciple is a person whose every thought, word and deed flow out of a heart that

---

8. Sinclair, *Biblical Discipleship*, 1.
9. Wagner, *Strategies for Church Growth*, 52.

desires to please God. A disciple is personally a learner, a follower of his master, and is therefore becoming like Christ." Lowrey also asks the question, "To what end are we discipling people?" His answer:

> "We are to be discipling people to be followers of Jesus Christ. Our aim is to move them into an ever closer personal relationship with him as their Lord and Teacher. Disciple making is not intended for a select group in the church, but for the entire congregation from the youngest infant to the oldest member. We do not 'arrive' as disciples."[10]

Pastor Lowrey is known as a genius in the area of campus ministry, a domain with considerable personal discipleship, and today he serves as a Christian educator with Great Commission Publications. His emphasis is always upon the heart of the follower. Notice the words "desire" and "please" in his definition. Following Jesus should supernaturally touch our core being in such a way that we become more like him in our heart-driven character. It's all about relationship; it is a continuous, unfinished work in progress. While we may mature as followers, we never reach a point in which we no longer need to grow, change, or deepen our walk with Christ. Discipleship has no age limits; all believers and their children are responsible to follow Christ. Everyone should draw closer to Jesus and follow him in thought, word, and deed, motivated by the heart.

A Recipient of and Responder to Grace

Finally, I would like to submit my own definition of a disciple of Jesus, one that I hope is full orbed,

> A Christian disciple is one who by God's grace has become a learner, a lover, and a follower of Jesus Christ. This follower is one who walks by faith in relationship with the risen Christ, and whose mind, emotions, and will are submitted to and changed by Christ's Word and his Spirit. The disciple obediently loves the triune God more and more, is becoming conformed to Christ's likeness, and grows in service to his body, the church. The process of discipleship occurs in the community of Christ's church and involves multiple and various avenues of influence—people, home life, activities, personal experiences, ministries outside of the church—in such a way that Jesus Christ uses "all of life" to sovereignly work

---

10. Lowrey, *The Primacy of Making Disciples*.

in his disciple's life in order to glorify his heavenly Father. When a person becomes engaged in this process with another individual, he is simply "investing" in the discipling work that Jesus himself is doing in that individual's life.[11]

After reading and analyzing all of the definitions of discipleship above, one would find difficulty in adding anything new to the thoughts previously expressed. However, I would like to stress that the whole person is impacted and that this change is initiated by God's grace.

Will Metzger, in his perceptive book on the topic of evangelism, *Tell the Truth*, provides an excellent explanation of how coming to Christ includes heart change in all three domains of the person. True conversion involves the mind (understanding the gospel), the emotions (feeling one's need, as well as the amazing provision of grace found in the gospel), and the will (new life and choices because of the gospel). If the whole being isn't changed, one can surmise that the person is not actually converted.[12] Similarly, discipleship or growth in Christ includes all of these domains. I recognize that each domain may express itself in different degrees (sometimes knowledge and learning rules; other times emotions, actions or activity appear to be the dominant attribute of the disciple), but if one of the three domains is not being developed, one should conclude that spiritual growth is being stunted or possibly that true conversion has never occurred.

I also want to emphasize in my definition that the disciple walks by faith, believing and trusting God to work in and through her life as she looks heavenward for hope, and also deals with reality in today's world. We experience the presence and fellowship of the living God and by faith walk hand-in-hand with him. This walk of faith is buttressed by the wonderful assurance that the believer walks in relationship with the risen Christ. His presence is our strength and life, the reservoir upon which we draw for daily sustenance. In addition to these thoughts, I believe it is very important to realize that *submission* to Christ is essential to the growth of the believer.

The true disciple lives constantly by the prayer Christ spoke in the garden of Gethsemane, "Not my will, but Yours be done." The follower is wholly devoted and reliant upon both the Word of God and the leading, guiding, and empowering presence of the indwelling Holy Spirit. Using the means of grace with full reliance upon the work of the Holy Spirit is absolutely necessary for any follower of Christ to grow. Ultimately, the Trinity

11. Culbertson, *The Disciple Investing Life*, xvii.
12. Metzger, *Tell the Truth*, 68–83.

is involved in the process of discipleship, with God the Father initiating the work graciously, Christ the Son providing the means for conversion (the cross), and the Holy Spirit converting the heart and doing his good and perfect work, while moving the believer toward Christ-likeness, all to the glory of God. Obedient love for the triune God is paramount as many who identify with the Christian life often neither define God as he truly reveals himself (the Trinity), nor follow him according to his word and will. The true outcome or fruit of discipleship is service to the body of Christ: more specifically, to Christ's body as expressed in the local church. Parachurch discipleship and ministry falls woefully short of the biblical goal of maturity if the local church is left out of the equation, whether inadvertently or not.

Furthermore, there is not only an organic dimension to discipleship that includes the influence of the lives of the people of God in his church upon the individual disciple, but there are sovereignly ordained avenues that enter the life of the disciple and form them in often profound ways. These avenues can include one-time encounters with another person, hearing a sermon on the radio, or a Christian-based song on the internet, or a choral presentation proclaiming the gospel, undergoing a mercy need that enters her life, or a multitude of other encounters and opportunities for spiritual growth. These providential circumstances and instances are designed by our heavenly Father in order to work his good pleasure into our lives so that Christ is formed in our hearts and he is glorified. The ultimate goal of discipleship is a life lived wholeheartedly for the glory of the triune God!

2

Recognizing a Disciple

HAVING DEFINED THE MINISTRY of discipleship, or "disciple investing" as I prefer to call it, we must now consider what a disciple of Christ looks like in today's world. The reality from Scripture is that a disciple or follower of the Lord today actually looks similar to a follower of the Lord (Yahweh) as described in the Old Testament. I want to take a cursory look at a short Old Testament passage since the Lord expressed very high standards for the people who would follow and represent him in the nation of Israel. His calling involved both heart and life!

What are the Attributes of a Disciple?
The Old Testament Speaks

The Lord God has always called out a people to follow him. He has not done so without giving them explicit guidance. Of course, his original call to the Hebrew nation to be his special and beloved people included an immediate provision of his moral will as communicated through the Ten Commandments. He also gave them many other mandates to help them maintain their holy calling as his chosen people. The gospel of God's grace (especially the reality of his forgiveness and pardon) can be found in the Old Testament in many passages, as can his expectations for his followers. Much can be learned from God's explicit instructions to his chosen ones. We ought never to view Old Testament believers as simply a law-driven people who responded to their deliverer with only rote and perfunctory obedience. Their Savior was always concerned about their hearts' willingness to give their loyalty and obedience to him.

I would like to look briefly at *one* prominent passage from the Old Testament that provides extensive insight into the calling that God places upon his followers after he delivers them from Egyptian bondage. Moses delivers this Scripture to the second generation of those who were saved from slavery to Pharaoh. Their parents, in flagrant rebellion and disobedience (Num 11–12), perished in the wilderness wandering. But God still had his people. This second giving of the law underscores what type of disciples or followers the living God desires.

This beautiful passage is from the Old Testament book of Deuteronomy, a book filled with wonderful instructions for those who would follow the true God in a world filled with idols and false gods. Here we discover the attributes of a [Christian] disciple,

> "And now, Israel, what does the Lord your God require of you, but to *fear* the Lord your God, to *walk* in all his ways, to *love* him, to *serve* the Lord your God with all your heart and with all your soul, 13 and to *keep* the commandments and statutes of the Lord, which I am commanding you today for your good?"[1]

These characteristics may be summed up as "one who *fears* the Lord, *walks* in all his ways, *loves* him, *serves* him with all of his heart, soul, mind, and strength and *observes* his commands and decrees." These five qualities would transform both the believer and the church if her people would only take these descriptors to heart.

Fear

I believe the first verb is the most crucial word in the string of verbs contained in this Scripture. "To *fear* the Lord" should be the driving force of every believer. A. W. Tozer states in *The Knowledge of the Holy*, "The greatness of God rouses fear within us, but His goodness encourages us not to be afraid of Him. To fear and not be afraid—that is the paradox of faith."[2] The true follower of Jesus is motivated by the greatness of his God—this is a reverence, regard, and respect in the heart for the Lord that is deeply embedded. What is this fear of the Lord? The greatest resource I have discovered, and one that succinctly explains a biblical view of the "fear of the Lord" is found in the final chapter of Dr. John Murray's classic text on Christian

---

1. Deuteronomy: 10: 12–13.
2. Tozer, *The Knowledge of the Holy*, 90.

ethics, *Principles of Conduct*. In the chapter entitled "The Fear of God," Dr. Murray defines the fear of God as "awe, reverence, honour, and worship." He states, "the fear of God is the soul of godliness."[3] Applying it personally, he writes, "The fear of God in us is that frame of heart and mind which reflects our apprehension of who and what God is, and who and what God is will tolerate nothing less than totality commitment to him."[4] He also says, "The highest reaches of sanctification are realized only in the fear of God (cf. 2 Cor 7:1)."[5] Furthermore, "But whatever the reason, the eclipse of the fear of God, whether viewed as doctrinal or as attitude, evidences the deterioration of faith in the living God."[6]

Dr. Murray breaks down the concept of the fear of God into these helpful categories:

A. There is the all-pervasive sense of the presence of God (God consciousness and relationship to him).

B. There is the all-pervasive sense of our dependence upon him and responsibility to him.

C. There is trust in his promises and providence (faith spawns obedience).

D. "It is the apprehension of God's glory that constrains the fear of his name. It is that same glory that commands our totality commitment to him, our totality trust and obedience."[7]

To properly fear the Lord as the almighty, sovereign, holy, creator God of the universe is the first and grandest attitude of the serious follower of Jesus Christ. I might suggest that the fear of the Lord is the starting point for any progress in growth as a disciple; thus, I have spent an extraordinary amount of space elaborating upon this obscure and rarely emphasized quality of the heart.

Walk

The Christian life is so often pictured in the Scriptures as a *walk*. The word *live* (*peripateo*) in the New Testament is also the word for *walk*. The picture

---

3. Murray, *Principles of Conduct*, 229, 236.
4. Ibid., 242.
5. Ibid., 231.
6. Ibid., 241.
7. Ibid., 242.

is one of step-by-step progress: slow, methodical, forward-moving progress done by faith. This is indeed the portrayal of discipleship, whether as an Old Testament saint (did they ever understand walking) or a New Testament believer who is trusting in the one who came and revealed the Father. The follower of Christ faces the continual grind of daily life and prepares to face each new sunrise as a forward-moving walk, and more importantly, takes those baby steps of faith knowing that ultimately, the Savior is holding his hand.

Love

The Christian life, and indeed the life of the disciple of Christ, is a life that resonates with love. First and foremost, this love must be a deep love for the Lord, not simply being in love with an ill-defined concept of love. We love because he first loved us. The Apostle Paul recognized that the love he had for the Lord, particularly for the saints and extending even unto the many lost and needy souls in the world, was a love derived from God through Christ, "For the love of Christ controls us . . . " (2 Cor 5:12). Until we comprehend God's love for us—a love that exists in spite of the fact that we were his enemies, ungodly, and sinners—and have experienced a love so deep that it required Christ's sacrifice on the cross—we cannot exude the love of God for others from the heart.

Service

Christian discipleship always results in the creation of *servants*. The Christian disciple's motto should inevitably reflect the words of Jesus found in the gospel of Mark, "For even the Son of Man came not to be served but to serve, and to give his life as a ransom for many" (Mark 10:45). Some scholars believe that this verse is the summary or key verse of the entire gospel of Mark, as the author's theme is to demonstrate that Christ came as a man in order to serve and die for humanity. In order for a disciple of Christ to live for the glory of God, he must learn to be a servant. This service is displayed in the local congregation (or the local church), in the community, as well as in the world, particularly among the broken and those needing mercy.

Servanthood flows both out of one's understanding of God's greatness and being, as well as his worthiness. It also flows out of the realization of Christ's own condescension to earth in order to procure our salvation.

The Apostle Paul clearly reinforces this concept from the example of Christ himself,

> "Have this mind among yourselves, which is yours in Christ Jesus, ⁶ who, though he was in the form of God, did not count equality with God a thing to be grasped, ⁷ but emptied himself, by taking the form of a servant, being born in the likeness of men. ⁸ And being found in human form, he humbled himself by becoming obedient to the point of death, even death on a cross."[8]

And according to the passage in Deuteronomy, this spirit of servanthood is not simply a dutiful, obligatory activity. Whenever and wherever we serve the Lord, it is to be with all of our hearts and souls.

Obedience

The final quality exhibited by the follower of the Lord is that of *obedience*, i.e., observing or keeping the commands of the Lord. Reading through this list, it is difficult to imagine that even in this Old Testament context, as the "next" generation prepares to enter the promised land, this attribute would be seen as legalistic and perfunctory. The fear of the Lord is a heart attitude, love for the Lord is an inner attitude, and service to the Lord is to be wholehearted and full of one's soul. Surely, their obedience was as the obedience of any disciple of Jesus should be: motivated by a grateful heart.

The bigger context of this passage is set in the reality of salvation, i.e., the exodus of the children or people of God out of Egypt, a beautiful drama of salvation in their lives. The follower of Christ, living in his grace, is always wondering how to please the Lord in daily life. And the desire to grant the Father pleasure is demonstrated by expressions of trusting faith and sensitive obedience to his will. Jesus taught his disciples to pray, ". . . Your kingdom come, Your will be done, on earth as it is in heaven" (Matt 6:10). And as Jesus prepared to die and depart, he reminded his disciples, "Whoever has my commandments and keeps them, he it is who loves me. And he who loves me will be loved by my Father, and I will love him and manifest myself to him" (John 14:21).

I might also suggest that the natural consequence of "fearing, walking with, loving, and serving" the Lord would be heartfelt obedience. And if obedience was expected of the believer in those early days of God's

---

8. Philippians 2:5–8.

redemptive plan, one might expect an even greater response of obedience in the full light of salvation revealed to us by the cross of Christ. Appropriately, Jesus's Great Commission to "make disciples" appears to be an imperative in its intention and includes "teaching them to *observe* all that I have *commanded* you . . ." Disciples of Christ are commanded to teach obedience to Christ's commands and to be obedient followers of Christ as well. He is pleased when we demonstrate that we are, indeed, his obedient followers!

Conclusion

Ultimately, disciple investing is participating in the work of making disciples, a work that Jesus has initiated and is doing in his "called ones'" lives. Christ is still calling men and women, girls and boys to follow him, and he is still changing lives, one person at a time. He invites us to not only follow him but to become fishers of people. We are both fishers and disciple investors when we engage in the disciple making process *he* is doing, and that process is sure to occur when we invest ourselves in the lives of others! We need to continue to hear and heed his compelling call to each of us, "Follow me, and I will make you fishers of men." (Matt 4:19)

3

Paul's Perspective on Disciple Investing

As one surveys the practices of the Apostle Paul, noting the many disciple investing relationships he has, there is one key passage in Paul's writings that demonstrates the multifaceted nature of his method of disciple investing. This chapter is designed to take a brief look at Paul's perspective on disciple investing as derived from his deeply heartfelt appeal to the young believers in the area known as Galatia, as seen in Galatians 4:19–20.

In this passage, the Apostle Paul states the reality of the difficulties of disciple investing in a verse filled with pithy phrases. The Apostle is wrestling with a grave heresy that has surfaced in the Galatian churches, one that threatens these new believers' understanding of Christ's justifying work. Paul is astounded that these believers, before whom he so passionately portrayed Christ as crucified on their behalf and for their forgiveness, are falling into the false doctrine of adding self-accomplishment/self-righteousness to the finished work of Christ on the cross. In keeping with the themes above, he uses five distinct phrases in one heart-wrenching statement. He writes, "my little children, for whom I am again in the anguish of childbirth until Christ is formed in you! 20 I wish I could be present with you now and change my tone, for I am perplexed about you." Here we see five powerful aspects of the disciple investing effort.

Parenting: "My dear children . . ."

If there is one powerful analogy that describes the disciple investing endeavor, it is that of parenting children. Deep love is exhibited by truly caring parents and that love is based upon an unending affection and deeply bonded relationship with their children. Self-sacrifice is evident as are indescribable emotions for their offspring. Ownership is evident, i.e., ownership of the child's life and future. Positive possessiveness also exists, a proper possessiveness that is jealous with affection. There is a sense of begetting or birthing and the responsibility to cuddle, coddle, raise, and release. Who can describe all of the feelings and emotions that a loving parent has toward her child? Yet, in some way, Paul links disciple investing to this powerful relational bond, possibly the highest bond between two people outside of the bond of marriage between a man and woman. Paul sees himself as a parent of sorts to these wandering believers. They are his! They are dear! They are an offspring of sorts! And this expression comes directly from one who was indeed a "man's man!"

Pain: ". . . for whom I am in the pains of childbirth . . ."

How could the Apostle Paul understand the pains of childbirth? Most scholars believe that Paul was not or had never been married (although 95 percent of all Pharisees were married, so some think he had been married and his wife had died). We can't imagine Paul being on the scene for the birth of his relatives' or others' children; he makes no allusions to that experience. Yet, he is well aware of the reality that, since the fall of Adam and Eve, childbirth brings pain and difficulty.

I have watched four children come into the world firsthand. Through what was a very popular childbirth training method at the time (the Lamaze method), I was directly on hand for the birth of all my children. My wife, Cathy, must receive full credit not only for the carrying of our children, but for carrying them to full term. Throughout the pregnancies and actual birthing, she alone endured the pain and physical trauma involved. All I contributed was a little consoling. Even my presence at the birth of our children added to her pain at times (Lamaze didn't prepare me for my own impatience and sin in the midst of stressful situations). I share all that personal revelation to say I still cannot begin to imagine the pain, discomfort, and difficulty that carrying and giving birth to a child requires. Yet Paul seems to understand.

And for Paul, the "spiritual" birthing process of these recent believers is incomplete; he agonizes over the possible loss of those he has led into the

PAUL'S PERSPECTIVE ON DISCIPLE INVESTING

realm of God's grace. He feels like the birthing process hasn't been completed and his distress is deeply personal. The children (Galatian believers) haven't been fully born yet (into a liberating understanding of grace). Paul implies that the umbilical cord of independent reliance upon the completed work of Christ has not yet been severed. Paul also has not been able to detach himself from the spiritual lives of these fledgling believers, letting go of them with a sure confidence that they do trust in Christ alone for their salvation. And this sense of his "children's" instability causes him great pain and torment of heart. Paul, as a spiritual parent, feels for his children as if he were their birth mother. Disciple investing is about spiritual parenting.

Spiritual parenting requires constant surveillance of the well-being of young and growing believers. I experienced this spiritual parentage and oversight prior to getting married. When my wife and I started to date seriously (we were engaged two months after we became serious—I don't necessarily recommend that timeline), and it appeared that we might have a future together, she told me that first I must meet two special people in her life. She stated coyly, "they want to meet you and approve of you." These two people were a young married couple my wife had known for the past few years. They were not part of a "shepherding" (disciple control) type cult; they were, simply stated, my wife's spiritual parents. My wife was raised in a very churchgoing (Presbyterian) home, and did not hear or understand the gospel until middle school. Her "hearing" actually came through the youth ministry of another Presbyterian church in her town. Eventually, as she grew as a Christian, she became very close with a couple who were students at the time at the local Bible college. Having experienced minimal spiritual guidance from her natural parents, she was "adopted" by this couple. In an informal fashion, they became her spiritual parents. They befriended, loved, inspired, and encouraged her in her walk with the Lord. And although they had moved many miles and hours away from her hometown, their spiritual parentage continued. The umbilical cord may have been severed but the depth of the relationship remained. They felt compelled to watch out for the well-being of this special spiritual daughter of theirs. Those were their motivations for meeting this serious suitor. Paul was like this with the Galatian believers, feeling long-term nurturing pain over their lives, and over their spiritual and personal success. Every disciple investor should reflect similar emotions and sensitivities toward those with whom they are working. (And by the way, thankfully they approved of their spiritual daughter's choice in husbands!)

Purpose: ". . . until Christ is formed in you . . ."

For the Apostle Paul, there is only one goal in the disciple investing process: that Christ's followers become like and reflect Jesus Christ himself. It is interesting to note that the Apostle parallels the believer's grasp of the doctrine of justification by faith alone with the reality of what we might call Christ-shaping or Christ-likeness. The passage appears to build the case that as long as the Galatian believers are adversely affected by the Judaizers' heretical teaching, i.e., reliance upon the law for acceptance by God, they will not be formed into Christ-likeness. For the Apostle Paul, disciple investing is all about leading other believers to see Christ, seek Christ, know Christ, rely upon Christ, and become like Christ. Christ-centeredness and Christ-likeness are the grand motives in Paul's ministry, and the reason why his fears for the Galatian believers make his spiritual parenting of them so agonizing. The disciple investor wants disciples to find and rely upon Christ alone, both for their salvation and also for their sanctification. Danger only follows when a disciple begins to look away from Christ alone!

Presence: ". . . how I wish I could be with you now . . ."

The passion to be with people, to be by their side, to have a place of influence at the table of their lives, resonates in Paul's ministry. The Apostle Paul here underscores his commitment to being directly involved in the lives of his disciples. The word *presence* speaks of *being at one's disposal*. How the Apostle Paul desired to be personally available in the lives of these believers! This is disciple investing at its best—being with the person/people you are seeking to build up. Robert Coleman, in his classic work (and one that I highly recommend), *Master Plan of Evangelism*, addresses this key concept in his chapter entitled "Association." Jesus's plan for reaching the world, Coleman proposes, was simply to spend an inordinate amount of time being with his small group of followers known as the twelve disciples.

I believe that while involved in what I call disciple investing, the greatest joys, deepest pleasures, and most longstanding relationships have been derived from those with whom I have spent the most amount of personal time. Each of them would have to speak for themselves about their own views of my presence in their lives; yet, I would submit from my own vantage point, that my being with them changed both the nature of the relationship for the better, and solidified the depth of the relationship for years to come. The Apostle Paul, in the midst of the Galatian crisis, is absolutely convinced that his presence on the scene—his influence, teaching, and caretaking—would make the difference for their souls. Woody Allen once stated, "80% of success is just showing up." I have found that statement (or premise) to be true in ministry. Disciple investing is simply "just showing up" in the lives of people in their time of need, people whose real need is to know Christ more, and then watching God work through your commitment to them and through the powerful means of grace he provides.

Perplexity: ". . . and change my tone, because I am perplexed about you."

One cannot emphasize the benefits of the disciple investing process without recognizing the stark reality of the difficulties that being involved in the lives of others brings. Ministry is laborious in and of itself, and the disciple investing process may be even more laborious. Disciple investing, as well as any committed involvement in other people's lives, will include facing a number of discouraging possibilities such as disappointment, failure, rejection, arrested development, and possibly a flight response by your disciple. The Apostle Paul had poured his life into the Galatian believers and he passionately reminded them of this fact throughout his letter to them.

Here he appears as a somewhat distraught parent who has given his all in guiding his children, only to see them tempted to make the worst of decisions. In this case the worst decision is life (and soul) threatening. Will they be adherents to the doctrine of justification by grace alone or will they cling to a semblance of justification by grace plus works? Their spirit of ambivalence towards the gospel has made Paul forceful, sharp, and direct in his tone toward them. Considering all the energy, effort, and sacrifice he has demonstrated to them, he is perplexed that they would so easily listen to the voices of false teaching and become enslaved to a theology of works righteousness (grace plus works for salvation). The disciple investor must make both Christ and the message of grace their primary focus. If they do, at times they will become perplexed by those who return to the message of self-effort and works for acceptance before God. And sadly, despite their best efforts, the disciple investor will experience some very perplexing shifts in thinking and behavior from even the best followers of Christ.

4

The Process: Influences in Disciple Investing

IN THIS CHAPTER, I wish to describe what I call "Three Tiers of Influence" in the disciple investing process. My premise for the following observations is that whether young or old in the faith, all believers are molded by three different avenues of influence in their walks with Christ. I will list these influences in the order of *least* impact, though depending upon an individual's relationship with the local church, the order might be reversed or affected in other ways. I might also add that I am indebted to Dr. Richard Pratt (at one time, an RTS professor), who taught these concepts in the (now defunct) RTS Distance Education course entitled "Introduction to Theological Studies" (if you can find it, listen to it!) I have laid out the Three Tiers as follows:

Influence Number One: One's Church (*Denominational*) Tradition

One can be confident that no matter what particular church one attends, that church is part of a bigger church, or a religious or denominational *heritage*. Even if said church considers itself "independent," it would not be difficult to discover the long-standing church traditions of belief, conviction, and practice that have formed that church's present identity. Rather than attempt to define the many church traditions, or analyze the formation of denominations, I would simply state that church history has recorded multiple expressions of commitment to the "systematic" teaching(s) of the Scriptures. These expressions can be recognized by the following popular categories: covenantal, dispensational, Arminian, Calvinistic, pietistic, "high church" liturgical, Wesleyan, Charismatic, Pentecostal, Baptistic, Catholic, Orthodox, Lutheran, Anglican, Episcopalian, Methodist, Holiness, Fundamental, Conservative, Evangelical, Liberal, Mainline, Anabaptist, Independent, pre-millennial, etc. Obviously, this is a long list of categories, and each and every one of them can influence the church that a believer attends.

The denominational label often speaks explicitly of the belief system and practices (or at least implies something) of the church's heritage and tradition. There exists an "historical theology" that either dominates, or at the least, rubs off on the respective church that the individual disciple of Christ is attending. This influence extends to such frameworks as church creeds and written confessions of faith, views on the church's expectations, and practices of the followers of the faith (church members), and in essence the explicit or implicit liturgies or worship practices or style. Usually there is some type of systematized theology that influences, or is foundational for, everything that the denomination or the heritage believes and inculcates into its members or adherents.

The biggest question facing the disciple investor is whether there is a religious tradition that affects the person she is discipling, and whether residual effects from that tradition remain in the life of the disciple. Sensitivity to present realities due to past influences is an appropriate attitude to maintain when investing in the life of another. The disciple investor should not spend the bulk of her time in the disciple investing process denigrating a religious tradition. I believe that she should both capitalize on the fact that the disciple has been influenced by a religious tradition and glean what she can from that tradition's influence. The disciple investor should also take that knowledge and begin pouring into the other person's life with all of the proper teachings of Scripture in order to overcome any adverse effects of the person's religious tradition. Nevertheless, one's religious tradition or background does influence disciple investing.

Reality is one reason why a person involved in the disciple investing process would do well to study various church, denominational, and religious traditions, and should develop a working knowledge of church history when possible. This knowledge would be beneficial in making one aware of potential false teaching, legalistic practices, and hierarchical or heavy-handed practices that may have shaped the individual being discipled in the past. Of course, many disciple investors will be younger

Christians who may be unaware of big picture traditions, theological distinctions, and various philosophies of ministries, and some may be resistant to the idea of traditions previously experienced. But despite this possible deficiency of knowledge, she will still be used by God to help others grow in their walks with Christ.

Ideally, the disciple investing process should be initiated and maintained by those with a mature or maturing understanding of the many aspects of the Christian faith. Illustrations for the very practical implications of this principle are numerous, but let me share just three possible scenarios:

A. The new believer/young Christian being discipled has grown up in an independent (or denominational) fundamentalist tradition that focused on keeping man-made rules as a proof of faith/belief, or as an attempt to maintain one's security in salvation. Such an emphasis normally falls under the rubric of "legalism," or the finding and/or maintaining acceptance with God through outward behavior or external rituals and practices. This tradition is not only rampant in sectors of evangelicalism but is notorious for debilitating faith-based and grace-based living. The disciple investor would again attempt to diagnose the disciple's background and their thinking as related to gospel-based living. One would need to focus on the nature of grace and/or the tension of grace and law, as well as address Christian freedom.

B. The new believer (or the young Christian) being discipled has been raised under the influence of the Roman Catholic tradition. Ultimately, the great flaw (among others, in my opinion) of this historic tradition is the meshing of justification with sanctification, or in simpler terms, reliance upon good works for acceptance with God rather than fully relying upon acceptance by God through the finished work of Christ on the cross (grace). The disciple investor would attempt to diagnose this possible misunderstanding—one that leads to frustrated efforts in Christian living, a sense of failure, and a certain lack of assurance of salvation. Then, using Scripture (the books of Galatians or Romans, for instance) he would clarify the biblical position of "justification by faith alone" with the disciple.

C. The new believer/young Christian being discipled grew up in a Reformed tradition that gravitated toward passivity in the Christian life due to an extreme emphasis on the sovereignty of God. This believer fails to take initiative in living out the Christian life, doing ministry with others, and neglects to attempt evangelism because he believes God has predestined everything that happens; thus, human efforts are inconsequential. Again, without overly criticizing the detrimental aspects (or conclusions) of this theological system or perspective, the disciple investor is committed to helping the disciple study the Scriptures in order to discover that God's sovereignty is not only *not* in conflict with the doctrine of the responsibility of humankind, but that contrary to human logic, the doctrine of sovereign grace actually spawns cheerful gratitude, grateful obedience, and inspired, passionate love and service to God and man.

Influence Number Two: One's *Local* Church

Disciple investing should occur as a fact of life in the local church. However, any astute observer recognizes that often, the last place that intentional one-on-one disciple investing can be found is within the local church. My belief is that if a person is hearing the Word of God preached or taught, that person is being discipled by Christ. This form of discipleship might be termed organic or systematic since the person is growing due to a greater understanding of Christ, and the Scriptures, based on experiences derived from both a teaching platform and a corporate (or community) environment that contributes either directly or indirectly to their progress in the faith. Whether the disciple is growing inside of the local church or outside of it (in a parachurch-type ministry), the local church will often have a large influence in a disciple's shaping and formation. The origins of this shaping arise from the following sources:

The Local Church Pastor

Since the pastor often sets the tone for the philosophy of the ministry of the church and frequently leads by preaching, he (or she, in growing instances) is potentially discipling all of the members or regular attendees of the church. Simply think of the great need for and power of Spirit-filled expository, as well as Christ-centered, grace-focused, God-honoring, and biblically practical preaching. And then compare it to the many alternatives: i.e., self-help, storytelling only, and topical and dialogical conversational messages or homilies. The conclusion is obvious for those who have experienced both. Very few people are converted or discipled by the latter, while the former shakes many people to the core of their being, draws them to God, and helps them grow in every aspect of the Christian life. The pastor of the local church, through preaching and a well-defined philosophy of ministry, has the real potential to set the stage and the standard for the disciple investing ethos of the congregation. Word-based and Christ-centered pastoral ministry can be transformational as the Holy Spirit blesses.

The Practices of the Church

A written or articulated philosophy of ministry is one thing, but how it plays out in the life and ministry of the church is another. The local church and its members should be expected to practice what they preach, or at least practice what the ordained leadership of the church teaches. A member of a local church is going to be heavily influenced by the behavior and activities of their respective church. If the church is to maintain a loving environment, the disciple will most probably learn how to love and be loved. If the church is committed to serving, the disciple will serve. If the church loves to learn, the disciple will learn. The church has a personality, as we shall see below, and that personality will (as most personalities do) draw or repel others. If drawn to the church's personality, the person who commits themselves to a specific church will be formed by that church's practices. The body of Christ is a powerful factor in the life of a disciple, one that is often underrated in its effect upon its members. The use of the means of grace within the community of Christ is metamorphic in the believer's life as the Spirit moves. The disciple investor would be wise to understand the context of the local church in the life of the person being discipled. Of course, that context would include all of the church/denominational traditions mentioned above, but each church brings with it heavy influences that shape the convictions of its followers.

The Church Personality: The Five Areas of Ministry (Philosophy of Ministry)

According to the book of Acts, the newly formed church displayed many distinct qualities that gave it both life and a magnetic radiance that was obviously from God. Luke describes these church traits when he writes,

THE PROCESS: INFLUENCES IN DISCIPLE INVESTING

> [42] And they devoted themselves to the apostles' teaching and the fellowship, to the breaking of bread and the prayers. [43] And awe came upon every soul, and many wonders and signs were being done through the apostles. [44] And all who believed were together and had all things in common. [45] And they were selling their possessions and belongings and distributing the proceeds to all, as any had need. [46] And day by day, attending the temple together and breaking bread in their homes, they received their food with glad and generous hearts, [47] praising God and having favor with all the people. And the Lord added to their number day by day those who were being saved.[1]

From this passage, we see what is known as the Five Areas of Ministry of the church. Understanding that the foundation of all ministry is prayer (42), the five areas described are:

1. Teaching/Education (42) "And they devoted themselves to the apostles' *teaching* . . ."
2. Fellowship/Community (42, 44) "And they devoted themselves to the apostles' teaching and the *fellowship* . . ."
3. Mercy/Ministry (44–45) "And they were selling their possessions and belongings and *distributing the proceeds to all*, as any had need."
4. Worship/Corporate Praise (47) "And day by day, attending the temple together . . . *praising God* . . ."
5. Evangelism/Conversion Growth (47) "*And the Lord added to their number* day by day those who were being saved."

It is my contention that although every local church is responsible for fulfilling all five of these areas of ministry, each particular church tends to thrive at doing two of these distinctions well. (I think the same is true of both individual Christians and Christian traditions and/or denominations.) Churches reflect their strengths, philosophy, vision, mission, foci, and their efforts based upon at least two (or three) of these five areas. There is only so much a church can do well. I believe this to be an accurate and helpful assessment and assumption. In essence, those two areas reflect what I call the church's "personality."

We observe church personalities all the time. Sometimes this observation reveals itself through complaint: we see weaknesses and shortcomings

---

1. Acts 2:42–47.

when a church fails to emphasize the ministries we value. Other times, we note the church's personality with a sense of pride (particularly our own), believing our church to be singularly gifted with Bible teaching, reaching the community, or loving each other, etc. As a matter of fact, I personally believe that our own (personal) strengths[2] draw us to the church that reflects our valued strengths. I'm not sure this is always a good practice, but it is a natural one. The point I am trying to make is that when you begin the disciple investing process in another person's life, there is a real possibility that the disciple will either reflect his own church's personality traits, or will gravitate toward those traits at the expense of others. A common example might be that of a new Christian (i.e., possibly an introverted intellectual) who was won to Christ through a loving (fellowship/community driven) church that is steeped in mercy ministry. He begins to grow in knowledge and doctrinal understanding and is consequently drawn to another church, one whose personality displays a heavy teaching ministry suited just for him. In the process however, he loses his zeal for evangelism and outreach, ironically forgetting the very principles and practices that brought him to Christ.

Patterns and Traditions of the Local Church

When a church holds to, or builds a tradition that guides its regular practices, there is very little possibility that those traditions will change overnight. Usually, the leaders will work to ensure that the church upholds these esteemed and valued beliefs and practices. As these traditions become the very fabric of the church and are maintained by the leadership, one can observe patterns of predictability in the life of the church. These patterns might be seen in the way the worship service is designed, or in the way the Sunday School program is run. It could possibly be the manner of the decision-making process, or the way that members are cared for and shepherded. The possible church patterns are almost endless; and with patterns come expectation and predictability. Through the process of predictability, traditions gain sway over church members and regular attendees. As a matter of fact, these patterns may be why most people attend their church of choice.

As part of the church ethos, these traditions are very strong disciple shaping factors. For good or for bad (and usually for good, if based on the Scriptures), these traditions can make a powerful impact in the life of a

---

2. Name your two strongest areas of ministry from the five listed above.

believer. This shaping factor should not be discounted by the disciple investor, and just as one's church tradition or denomination should be considered when pouring into another person, so should their local church, assuming that they have had one. Diagnosis of the disciple's church background is an easy starting point for the disciple investor and provides plenty of springboards for addressing spiritual needs. I will speak to that further under the category "Diagnosis" below.

Influence Number Three: One's *Personal* Preferences

As mentioned above, each tradition or denomination, and each local church has its own personality. The same is true for each individual disciple. Without going into a psychological assessment or deep individual analysis, the disciple investor needs to ask some very pertinent questions about the disciple's understanding of himself and his ministry "personality" (the five areas of ministry in his own life). Which of the five areas does he gravitate toward? What are his weaknesses in practice and in understanding? Other questions should be posed about any or all of the categories covered in what would be called "systematic theology" (more on that subject later). Is this person a thinking type, a feeling type, or an active doer? These personal preferences often draw the disciple to a particular church or church tradition. Finally, the disciple's comprehension of the Scriptures as well as his application to daily life and personal issues is another relevant area of spiritual inspection.

The Priesthood of the Believer

One of the reasons for delving into the disciple's personal understanding is to both develop and encourage the concept of "the priesthood of the believer" in the disciple's life. Is the disciple learning how to read, study, meditate over, and interpret God's Word in such a way that helps him live the Christian life with Christ as Lord and with Scripture as the infallible guide for his life? Is the disciple learning to glean from God's Word and making some of his own Spirit-led decisions through the wisdom he has gained from his study of those Scriptures? Is the disciple learning to walk with Christ in such a way that he can personally draw upon Christ as his leader and guide?

Personal Convictions

Related to the topic of the priesthood of the believer is the development of the disciple's personal convictions. Those convictions could be biblically based or unbiblical, but they need to be understood in order to address either the lack of understanding, the errors that might exist, or to clarify scriptural teaching. What does the disciple believe about basic Christian doctrine? How convinced is she about that doctrine? And how strong is her adherence or submission to it? Inquiry about personal convictions is a natural segue to the topic of Christian liberty. For example, the disciple investor might ask: "What are the (black and white) issues to which you hold strongly?" "When and where are you uncertain about specific practices in the Christian life?" "How does your tradition/denomination and/or your local church's practices (personality) and convictions affect or influence your convictions?" If you like theology and delving into how a person's real-life affects their actions and behavior, this process of personal questioning is actually quite interesting and enjoyable. I might even describe it as a fun aspect of ministry that can be very rewarding.

Personal Experiences

People always bring the past baggage of sin into their present lives, whether those sins are of their own making, or consist of another's sins against them. These may be very tragic realities and wounds so deep that at times they are beyond words of expression. These are painful and life-changing experiences that the disciple investor needs to explore. Disciple investing is a time for personal questions concerning whether change in the disciple's life is truly going to occur. We must be honest before the Lord and before others about the personal problems we experience (often on a daily basis), and the apparent reasons for those problems. Along with personal baggage, every believer has some secret sin or some nagging temptation that simply seems to be impossible to overcome. Patterns or habits of sin in a given area create a sort of entrenchment of sin in the deep recesses of a person's heart. These habits need to be lovingly exposed and dealt with. Only when these sins (often addictive and enslaving habits of sinful brokenness) are confessed, repented of, and placed on the cross can the disciple know forgiveness and gain any victory over them and the guilt and shame they bring.

Confession comes from transparency and transparency comes from trust. Sharing each other's personal lives and struggles becomes a conduit of personal transformation, because in a genuine disciple investing relationship, trust is preeminent. A one-on-one context is the perfect setting for asking real questions about real-life experiences, especially those that are or have been powerful soul shapers. One can ask a multitude of questions, but it is best to refrain from jumping too deeply into the other person's private life until the trust relationship is so strong that open sharing seems natural. Some disciple investors will be better suited at building a context of transparency than others, and each needs to understand his or her own gifts, personality, and limitations.

However, at times an intense conversation can ensue unexpectedly. This is due to the fact that, unknown to the disciple investor, the individual has been waiting to find someone with whom he may confide and now is the time and opportunity. People sometimes live with very dark secrets (more so now than in the past I believe, due to the effects of rampant sexual immorality) and often cannot deal or live with the guilt and/or awareness of what they've done, experienced, or become. One can readily see the relationship between entering into another's personal experiences and one-on-one counseling that occurs in disciple investing.

Growth in Understanding the Scriptures

As believers grow and mature in their knowledge of the Lord and the knowledge of God's Word, they develop convictions, or what are called "personal creeds/beliefs" (whether written or not). As described above, this belief system is most assuredly influenced and developed by their church and religious system; with the growth of biblical knowledge and instruction on a personal level, the disciple often brings his own developed thoughts and beliefs to bear when interacting with the disciple investor. Oftentimes, these convictions are based on a poor understanding of Scripture. Sometimes a disciple's thinking is a result of inadequate study or lack of exposure to and explanation of Scripture. A disciple investor might diagnose a person's level of biblical understanding via the following categories:

1. Has no knowledge whatsoever
2. Has knowledge of some basic concepts from the Bible
3. Acknowledges Old and New Testament distinctions of some sort

4. Recognizes various Bible stories but sees little meaning in them
5. Knows Special passages (Genesis and the Creation account; Psalms 23; Matthew 6—the Lord's Prayer; John 3:16; Luke 15—the Prodigal Son; the book of Revelation means "the end times", etc.) but knows little else
6. Knows various books of the Bible and/or Bible characters but has no understanding of the "big picture" (historical/redemptive meta-narrative) of the Bible
7. Understands lots of facts about the Bible and books of the Bible but has no heart transformation
8. Has learned some basic "Sunday School" or Christian school information about theology and the Bible but the information is simply facts
9. Has lots of knowledge, but not necessarily good knowledge, inculcated by an overzealous church or even a cult
10. Has a solid grasp on basic evangelical (or denominational) doctrine and the Bible

Once the disciple's understanding of Scripture has been assessed, one can determine (with freedom and discretion) where to begin and how to address her needs on an individual basis. These needs must deal not only with knowledge, but also with the heart/affections and behavior. Such a diagnosis may prevent the disciple investor from falling into a programmatic response to needs and weaknesses, a response that often applies a rote and canned prescription to the problem. However, in many ways once the disciple investor is familiar with what the disciple knows (or doesn't know, which is usually the case), he has eons (as we used to say as children) of freedom to open up the Bible and deal with a multitude of subjects. I discuss some of those topics (or areas of discipleship) in my previous book, *The "Disciple Investing" Life*.

5

Disciple Investing Encounters

ONCE AN INDIVIDUAL BEGINS to pursue the ministry of disciple investing, he will encounter various responses from those whom he approaches. These responses are often indicative of the person's spiritual status. No matter how the disciple responds, the disciple investor will understand that he is beginning the process of diagnosis; all is not lost by an indifferent or otherwise undesirable response. Nevertheless, such responses need to be handled carefully so that manipulation and/or guilt do not become methods of forced cooperation. Responses such as these may indicate that the Holy Spirit is not moving in the person's life at the present time. If the disciple investor desires to move forward, he should do so prayerfully, seeking the Lord's guidance and wisdom, as well as patience for himself, knowing that God is sovereign in his work. Some examples of these responses/attitudes are as follows:

Non-Christian or false Christian (unbeliever)

Sometimes a person shows interest in the attention gained from the disciple investor but isn't really interested in Christ, the Scriptures, or real, personal spiritual growth. Sometimes the person appears to be a Christian but actually is not. True Christian faith is not always present even when there appears to be evidence of a Christian life; true Christian faith is not always discernible. However, in many ways this opportunity is one of the most exciting—particularly if the individual has a genuine sense or desire to learn and grow. The Holy Spirit may very well be moving in his life. You can certainly invest in another person *as if* he is a disciple of Jesus, even if he is not. Disciple investing is evangelizing in this case and is the first step (so to speak) in obeying Jesus's Great Commission to "go and make disciples." Simply explaining the gospel could become a powerful moment as the disciple investor watches this non-Christian disciple's eyes open wide to God's grace.

For example, during my sophomore year in college my freshman roommate was an apparent non-Christian although he had grown up in and experienced a rather good and somewhat conservative Presbyterian church. Being my roommate certainly granted me all manner of opportunities to talk about my new-found faith in Christ (I had become a Christian during the fall semester of my freshman year) and one might say that I was initiating the disciple investing process. We talked about questions of faith, the Bible, and Jesus, though the conversations were minimal. He revealed he was not a Christian, although he claimed to be when asked. However, he was willing to talk. I was discipling and evangelizing to him at the same time. He was not resistant to me, although he was resistant to my good friends in Campus Crusade for Christ (Cru) and had instructed me that he wanted to be left alone by them. However, before I could convey his wishes, they showed up one day while I was out and, using the *4 Spiritual Laws*, led him to faith in Christ. I walked in the door just before he asked Jesus Christ to enter his life. He would never be the same. When my friends departed from our room, my new Christian roommate was left with me as the only "mature" Christian he knew. I wasn't so sure about his "sinner's prayer" asking Christ into his life, so I went out and purchased him a brand new Living Bible (based on its simplicity) and gave him some good and helpful verses to read. The disciple investing process had only deepened because it had already begun when he was a non-Christian. How exciting for me to be a part of the process and to watch him literally enter into the kingdom of God! That day was one of the greatest highlights of my entire life!

Willing, but unsure or even intimidated

Jesus, as he faced the cross in the garden of Gethsemane, said to his sleeping and drowsy disciples, "The spirit indeed is willing, but the flesh is weak" (Matt 26:41). Oftentimes possible disciple investing candidates are willing but so unsure of what might happen that they simply cannot get started. Fear of commitment or fear of being transparent can be staggering blows to the psyche of a young or new believer in Christ. When approached, the individual agrees to make the effort and may sincerely exude hope in the possibility of spiritual growth and/or friendship with the disciple investor. However, the factor of intimidation can take over and as with any consideration of commitment, the person begins to realize the following potential concerns:

A. They don't know much and their lack of knowledge is going to be exposed

B. There will be demands and expectations for obedience on the part of the disciple

C. Faithfulness to the relationship and the task could be overwhelming (I have seen some discipleship programs that are far more demanding at the beginning than they ought to be)

D. Necessary spiritual disciplines (and the weakness of the flesh) may impact their life and schedule in a new manner of living

Needing Counsel

Often (and this is happening more and more) the disciple investor discovers that those willing to meet for regular help in spiritual growth are actually there to receive sustaining personal support, or what I might call counseling. Thirty years ago, as a campus minister at the University of Florida I was meeting one-on-one with numerous students on a weekly basis, always with the hope that spiritual (i.e., biblical) discussion would ensue. Oftentimes I carried a "spiritually focused" agenda, i.e., I had purposes and intentions to address a specific spiritual discipline or topic using a passage from the Scriptures to guide our conversation. However, many times as the student and I engaged in discussion, the time we spent together meandered away from my plan and centered around the needs of the student. The first few times this happened, being the goal-oriented person I am, I was internally frustrated. My initial conclusion was that I simply wasn't focused enough to stay on task. I allowed the student to divert me from my seemingly "Spirit-led" plan. However, in time I realized that the importance of the students' personal (and often daily) struggles far exceeded the agenda I brought to the conversation. Many students needed spiritual counsel and in reality, though I was not sitting down with them and walking through a passage of Scripture as I had planned, I was actually addressing their real needs by giving them counsel based on both the Scriptures and the truth (or theology) that I had to offer them.

Ultimately, I was providing a Christ-centered, grace-centered (with the appropriate application of the third use of the law—guidance), and Scripture-centered ministry to struggling Christian students, and God was using this approach despite my own failure to carry forth the meetings my way. Had I remained in a rigid ministry mode, I believe my ministry to students would have been hindered. One particular student leader comes to mind. Because he was a leader, we met regularly for check-ups, discussions, and of course my goals for scriptural study in mind. But it seemed that almost every time we met, the conversation turned to his personal struggles, whether with his studies, his emotions, his parents, his relationships, his girlfriend, his future, etc. As I loved on him, I disregarded my plans and we would simply sit together and just talk (not my style at all!)

Eventually he graduated from college. I conducted his wedding and then he (and his wife) moved on. Time passed. Years passed. Then one day, about ten years later, he called me out of the blue (we were hundreds of miles apart). He told me how grateful he was for helping him get through college and he just wanted to see how I was doing. That in itself was a blessing and I marveled with joy. More years passed and he called again. He was doing well, his family was doing well, he had a great job, and he was walking with the Lord. Then he said, "I wanted you to know that I have been diagnosed with an emotional disorder. I have had it all of my life. But thanks to you and our regular discussions, I survived college—you helped me to graduate!" Looking back, I realize that flexibility in my approach and adjusting my ministry style to include these counseling sessions had both become inevitable and necessary. It was after this second call that I fully understood that the listening I had done with him was the most valuable service I could have rendered to this young man at the time. Biblical counseling—the application of the Scriptures to the issues of life—is absolutely essential in the disciple investing process and more powerful than we can imagine, as the Holy Spirit uses the word in the lives of his followers!

Growing

Thankfully as the Holy Spirit moves in people's lives and they are truly converted, the most natural result is that individuals are ready to grow. "Like newborn infants, long for the pure spiritual milk, that by it you may grow up into salvation—³ if indeed you have tasted that the Lord is good" (1 Pet 2:2–3). Besides witnessing a true conversion to Christ, there is nothing more exciting than ministering to or investing in a brand new disciple who is ready to grow. In a way, most anything the disciple investor does is accepted and treated like gold. One of the most exciting aspects of disciple investing is the place of diagnosis in a believer's understanding of God's Word. Biblical illiteracy is sadly rampant today, even in the areas of the United States previously known as the Bible belt. And of course, much of the world has not been blessed with the proliferation of Bibles, churches, and ministries as has North America. If, as we believe, the Bible is the Word of God, and is the special revelation that God has provided for our redemption, salvation, justification, and sanctification, then the goal would be most certainly for every follower of Christ to grow in his knowledge of God's truth.

And nothing is much more enjoyable in the ministry of disciple investing than to open the word of God to someone who hasn't really read or heard the Scriptures taught, and to watch the awe that takes place when the Holy Spirit grants him enlightenment and understanding. The Scriptures are described as light and a lamp (Ps 119:105), milk (1 Pet 2:2), a sword (Heb 4:12), a mirror (Jas 1:23–25), water (Isa 55:10–11), fire and a hammer (Jer 23:29), and food or bread (Jer 15:16). Hebrews 4 also says the Word of God is alive and powerful. The combination of the power of God's Word and the ministry of the Holy Spirit powerfully applying the Word in the life of the believer guarantees that there will be a response to the will of God, a response that moves the believer toward Christ-likeness. This may not be measurable, but it is observable. Both conviction of belief and encouragement derived from a study of the Scriptures bring spiritual life and change to the believer. The key is simply starting, i.e., meeting together with someone and opening the Scriptures.

When my roommate prayed to ask Christ into his life (and it was powerful), I immediately went out and purchased a Living Bible for him. All I did to "disciple" him was merely give him a list of the best verses I knew— many were memory verses from the Navigator TMS (Topical Memory System)—that I had worked on during the past year as a new believer myself. In about thirty minutes he had read them all and said, "What's next?" Wow! And I was ready. I had been discipled to start a new believer in the gospel of John and then to consider Romans and James (practical living) as well as the Psalms. He jumped into the gospel of John, moved on to Romans and James, dabbled in the Psalms, and by the time his first semester was complete, he had read the entire New Testament. I didn't have to motivate or push him for one second. I just watched what the Holy Spirit was doing and was I ever impressed by *his* work! My college roommate was growing, his appetite for Scripture and knowing God was both insatiable and unquenchable. Who wouldn't want to do some disciple investing in that setting? Such is not necessarily the norm, but if new believers are truly converted, they will want to grow. The disciple investor experiences the pleasure of going along for the ride—an exciting one at that!

Maturing

The obvious goal in the disciple investing process is that the disciple moves toward a stage of development that could be called "a mature/maturing Christian." This is every pastor's or disciple investor's hope for those involved in his or her ministry. Paul writes about this important desire for those living underneath his ministry, "Him we proclaim, warning everyone and teaching everyone with all wisdom, that we may present everyone mature in Christ" (Col 1:28). Also, "Epaphras, who is one of you, a servant of Christ Jesus, greets you, always struggling on your behalf in his prayers, that you may stand mature and fully assured in all the will of God" (Col 4:12). Finally, mature thinking is a true sign of growth, "Brothers, do not be children in your thinking. Be infants in evil, but in your thinking be mature" (1 Cor 14:20).

Sometimes (and we would hope it were more often) the disciple investor encounters a believer who has been blessed with a solid Christian foundation in education and experience. The disciple has a keen understanding of Scripture, at least beyond the usual believer, and has previously been involved in the church and/or Christian ministry. This disciple has advanced beyond the essential and necessary basics of faith and is growing, or is at least willing to grow, in greater depth and understanding. Usually at this stage, the disciple is ready to go beyond her current understanding of the Bible and other theological concepts. She wants to grasp the deeper truths of Scripture, particularly categories such as systematic theology and the big picture redemptive implications of Scripture. The purpose and structure of the books of the Bible become more significant. Wrestling with the various concepts that deal with personal growth in Christ (sanctification) often surfaces within meaningful conversations. Seeking after victory in the Christian life and understanding the role of Christ's person and work grow in focus. Mortification (the putting to death) of sin, the place and role of the believer in ministry and in the church as well as spiritual giftedness, and leadership training become more meaningful topics.

This disciple is ready and eager to grow beyond her present reality, wishing to build upon the good foundation given her in previous churches or ministries. This person is often a pleasure to work with as long as she is teachable, humble, and non-combative. Contrariness can surface if this person feels that her knowledge base gives her personal spiritual advantages over other believers, particularly over the disciple investor (who may very well be lacking in some knowledge areas, in comparison to her friend).

Teaching

As alluded to above, a growing believer who is teachable doesn't necessarily want to teach or help others. However, depending upon one's calling and giftedness, the disciple investor has the grand opportunity of helping the fellow believer learn how to disciple others through the means of teaching. Teaching includes training (the next item below) and the disciple investor will need to have some skills and experience to pass along for the disciple's benefit. Every church and ministry needs capable, motivated, and qualified teachers since teaching is such a crucial aspect of the Great Commission.

It is only natural for the disciple investor, whether he is in a church or a parachurch ministry, to be looking for those growing disciples who are able, willing, and mature enough to teach others. The context can be a small group or a large group, as well as one-on-one teaching. Each teaching context has its own inherent challenges and requires special skill sets. Preparation for the disciple investor's teaching role is time well spent, for they can delegate responsibility and enable the ministry to grow, at least potentially, through another teacher. In reality, time spent with the disciple who is an aspiring teacher is a priority for the disciple investor. Caring for new ("baby") Christians is crucial and actually enjoyable in many ways, but focused investment in the disciple who can enhance the ministry and potentially lead is of uppermost significance. The disciple investor must capitalize on this blooming potential.

Training

The area known as training involves a multitude of responsibilities for the disciple investor. Oftentimes, the disciple investor is unable to put as much time into training as he put into helping the disciple learn and/or practice the spiritual disciplines necessary for personal Christian growth and sanctification. Training requires skills or knowledge of the task on the part of the disciple investor and also can require a lot of time. The acrostic, TDOEE[1] is helpful in order to understand the full scope of a good training process:

- Teach
- Demonstrate
- Observe
- Evaluate
- Encourage

Training begins with *teaching*, instruction, and understanding. The disciple must be given proper content and methodologies for communicating the truth to be taught. Facts and information are imperative. But information alone, though possibly adequate for some tasks, is often not enough. The disciple can learn by leaps and bounds if he is able to watch how teaching and other tasks are done. *Demonstration* is a powerful teacher. Yogi Berra, the paragon of nonsensical sense-making statements once stated, "You can observe a lot by just watching."[2] Mr. Berra was right on target when it comes to training disciples. They can observe a lot by just watching the disciple investor do and carry out whatever the task may be. Conversely, the disciple investor can learn a lot about how the disciple has "watched" by *observing* as well, i.e., observing how he fulfills the task or responsibility he has been given.

One can already see how time consuming the TDOEE process might become if done well. Those demands will continue as the disciple investor must *evaluate* the disciple, i.e., give actual, personal, and verbal feedback on how the disciple fulfilled the task or job. This aspect of TDOEE is the most difficult because each of us knows that critique often comes across as

---

1. Developed by InterVarsity Christian Fellowship and presented to me in my early Reformed University Fellowship—RUF—campus minister training.

2. Yelled out as the Yankee manager to his players who were in the game but not paying attention.

criticism. Though criticism is both unpleasant and usually poorly received by sane individuals, it must be done.[3] Evaluation naturally leads to the final stage of TDOEE which is to *encourage*. This step is essential; to overlook it will only create relational chaos, if not failure in the ministry task. Love is the chief motivator in the disciple investing process. Without it, performances can still sail, but with it those same sails become filled with gales of wind. If loving critique occurs, encouragement for accomplishments and efforts displayed needs to be doled out to the disciple as well.

Leading

There are teachers, there are trainees, and then there are leaders. Leaders can often teach (and can almost always communicate), but their gifts go beyond teaching and speaking. Leaders often work with trainees who can perform the most necessary tasks to make leadership successful (without which one cannot lead), but their gifts must supersede the basic ability to train. Leaders *must* lead. They must become the people who influence and change group behavior through the Lord's presence, power, and Spirit. It is difficult to explain what must be done to develop a leader. Leaders are often discovered as un-honed potential, but even when discovered they need to be refined, developed, and unleashed. In some ways, unleashing them provides a means of developing their leadership skills. The wise disciple investor will find and prescribe the appropriate setting for the development and exercise of the prospective leader's gifts and skills. Helping to shape a leader's abilities, if done well, is one of the great joys of the disciple investor, especially if the disciple investor is a pastor of a church who is building a team. Watching a leader blossom in a ministry team context for the profit of the church's ministry can be an indescribable blessing. The disciple investor is able to acknowledge the calling of the Lord in the disciple's life and gives thanks for the provision of a fellow servant in the Lord's work.

Reproducing

Many observers and proponents of the disciple investing process believe that any ministry that deals with finding, selecting, helping, developing,

---

3. Former University of South Carolina football coach Steve Spurrier was an expert at it and successful in his approach.

maturing, and training a disciple to lead reaches its height when the disciple is actually able to reproduce in a ministry context. In other words, the investment process reaches its zenith when the disciple becomes a disciple investor in any context of ministry. Reproduction does not have to look the same as that which brought the disciple to the point of maturity. The disciple can reproduce through teaching, one-on-one relationships, writing, children's ministry, camp ministry, administration, etc., as long as they are serving Christ and pouring themselves into kingdom-building.

There is nothing more exciting to the disciple investor than to watch (possibly over years of time) an individual in whom they have invested turn around and invest in others for Christ's sake and glory, no matter what the context. As the disciple grows and matures, the true disciple discovers God-given gifts and abilities that enables her to invest in and build up others in the faith. These gifts and abilities are expressed both inside and out of the local church and help grow other believers as well as God's kingdom. Quite possibly, the measure of the true effect of disciple investing is found in the disciples it produces, i.e., those who are able in turn to help others in their walks with God.

Summary

I will conclude this chapter simply by placing the "continuum" of receptivity to the disciple investor in order of less receptive to most so that one may see the various levels of need and investment.

- Non-Christian or false Christian (unbeliever)
- Willing, but unsure or even intimidated
- Needing counsel
- Growing
- Maturing
- Teaching
- Training
- Leading
- Reproducing

6

Spiritual Diagnosis[1]

Understanding People and Process

A LARGE PART OF the disciple investing process involves getting to know people and learning to wait on the Lord to do his work in their lives. Getting to know people occurs as we sincerely engage them, ask questions, listen to their answers and explanations with patience, and love them no matter what. We want them to understand the gospel, comprehend who God really is, see their own personal need, and embrace the cross of Christ as their only hope for this life and the life to come. Usually progress occurs slowly and does not exhibit itself in great measure unless a radical conversion to Christ takes place. Waiting on God to work is often necessary, but as we wait we can still, like John the Baptizer, point people to "the Lamb of God who takes away the sins of the world." Interestingly, a valuable part of pointing (for John it was preaching) is inquiring. Asking questions and discerning the answers is an intriguing means of not only getting to know others but learning the realities of their hearts and spiritual understanding. The means whereby the disciple investor builds a relationship that moves another toward Christ and the gospel involves asking questions, listening to revelations, making observations, and suggesting some biblical solutions. This process is what I call "spiritual diagnosis."

---

1. Some of these categories have been derived from the Staff Training notebook produced by Reformed University Fellowship, the campus ministry of the PCA; used by permission.

Sowing, Reaping, and Patience

Spiritual diagnosis is similar to the farming practice of sowing and reaping. We know that planting seeds and harvesting crops involves patient waiting. It can be exciting and nerve wracking, and it doesn't happen overnight. As a college student, I watched a number of people come to faith in Christ through a simple gospel presentation created by Bill Bright of Campus Crusade for Christ (Cru): *The 4 Spiritual Laws*. Many of these individuals had been prepared by interactions or encounters with other people (sowing) and were ready to trust Christ by the time they heard the gospel (reaping). However, as is often the case, the first time the disciple investor, or any believer talks to them, most people have not yet been prepared by God's Spirit to trust Christ. In many instances, God is pleased to use the slow and long process of sowing, watering, and reaping, which involves proclaiming the truth both in word and deed in the context of a trust-confidence relationship. Therefore, the disciple investor must be sensitive to the Spirit's work in the life of the individual.

Here are a few examples of this principle. When I was a campus minister at the University of Florida, I would frequently receive names of incoming freshmen students (and others) from churches across the state, both male and female. Usually these names were of students who were not eager to find a campus ministry of any sort; 90 percent of these students had no interest in following Christ on campus, as indicated by their responses. I know because over the years, I contacted every one of them I could find. Some met with me, most were courteous but not seriously interested in our ministry, and occasionally I was insulted by a truly disinterested student (one student sarcastically called me "holy father"). Nevertheless, I understood the mentality of freshmen students since I myself had gone off to college with the desire to get the Lord and all things Christian out of my life. As a campus minister, I knew that God would always be at work and that I should continue to sow seeds. Therefore, I made it a practice that after the first semester was over, I would contact at least some of these now second-semester freshmen students once more. I believed that through prayer and providential circumstances, God might have shaken up some of them. I discovered that often this was the case. The sowing that had taken place in their church upbringing eventually came to fruition. I had to give these freshmen time to face life as budding adults and realize that they could not make it on their own in college. God, through time and circumstance, had broken them to the point that they were now open to following him in a campus ministry. This turnaround was a rare one, but it did happen.

Another illustration happened in a church plant with which I was working. A young couple and their small son began to attend our church. They seemed to like us, even though we were not very large and were meeting in a local elementary school auditorium. Eventually, as was my practice when possible, Cathy and I took this couple out to dinner simply to get to know them a little better. We had a great meal; they were easy to converse with and they were very willing to speak about spiritual things—their interest was real and genuine. The husband however, was vague about his relationship with Christ. His background was Roman Catholic and his history of church attendance was sporadic. So, I took the opportunity to step out and ask him the first of the two common questions known as the "Evangelism Explosion" questions. The first question is, "Have you come to the place in your spiritual life where you know for certain that if you were to die tonight you would go to heaven?" He responded, "Yes, I think so." I had asked the question in the course of casual conversation and decided that now was not the time to pursue the second EE question (which asks why should God let you into his heaven). I let the inquiry lie for the time being. Nothing more was said at that time because I believed that this couple would continue to attend our church, continue to sit under the means of grace, and continue to hear gospel-centered and Christ-centered preaching. A couple of months went by. Then one day the husband sent me an email. He stated, "Rod I just had to let you know that I have become a Christian; I have trusted Christ as my Savior. I just wanted to thank you for asking me that question at dinner a few months ago. I know I said I thought I was going to heaven but I didn't really know. That question just dogged me forever. I could not get it off of my mind. I had to find the answer." Sowing, time, and patience. God is at work and we can trust him to build his kingdom in his own time and way. This is the power of diagnosis: helping people take stock of their spiritual lives, and then watching the Holy Spirit's wind blow to and fro, bringing God's elect into the kingdom!

Different Levels of Spiritual Maturity

Dr. Bill Hull, an expert in the field of discipleship, provides a helpful grid dealing with what he calls "Different Levels of Spiritual Maturity." The categories he mentions are insightful and should assist the potential disciple investor in the process of spiritual diagnosis. Dr. Hull is essentially answering the question, "Where is the person on the continuum of knowing Christ?" Below are his five helpful categories:

1. The Seeker: A seeker is any person who seeks meaning and answers in a religious context. We usually think of a seeker as unchurched. Most are looking for authentic spirituality, so they want to join and learn the new culture.

2. The Starter: A starter is a new disciple who is eager, willing, and naïve in the ways of church.

3. The Struggler: Strugglers have trouble working through difficulties.

4. The Stagnant: The stagnant people are stuck spiritually as a result of neglect. They neglect the practice of spiritual disciplines and choose to live off yesterday's manna—the doctrines and experiences from the past. Stagnant people can be very dangerous to the church because they tend to be unteachable and prone to complaining.

5. The Stable: The stable people are faithful and growing disciples. You can count on them to train, to give, to serve, to encourage, and to pray for others.[2]

As we think through these categories and discover the people who reflect them, we come to recognize that each one will need to be treated differently. Some (categories two and five) will excite us, as might category one because these people desire to grow, learn, and even serve. Others will pose challenges, potential frustrations, and require much patience and encouragement.

Another diagnostic tool that I have often used in the disciple investing process comes from the realm of counseling. In 1980, I took my final Master of Divinity seminary course with renowned Christian counselor and professor Dr. Larry Crabb. Dr. Crabb provided an extremely strategic methodology for personal and spiritual diagnostics in the area of counseling. His counseling diagnostic method consisted of "Four Circles," circles that represent what educators call the Three Learning Domains. In addition to these three, he added another crucial and viable category, the personal background circle. Although the Four Circles were designed for the purposes of counseling another person, I discovered, as a campus minister at the University of Florida with Reformed University Fellowship (RUF), that

---

2. Hull, *The Complete Book of Discipleship*, 256.

the Four Circles provided me with simple, easy-to-use categories for getting to know where students were coming from in both their personal and spiritual lives.

Consider the Four Circles:

1. Thinking—What does the person think about his problem and how to solve it? How does he think his problem was created or caused? What does he believe might be the answer? Does he have any biblically based answers or solutions? What does he think about God's role in solving the problem? What does he really believe about the gospel?

2. Emotions—How does he feel about his situation? Does he display any apparent emotions as he discusses the problem? How does he "feel" about getting out of his present or problematic situation?

3. Behavior—What are her challenges in life? When does she feel like she has made mistakes or poor decisions? What did she do to get herself into the problematic situation? What is her strategy for getting out of the situation (i.e., what does she plan to do next)? Is her plan of attack reasonable, workable, and biblical?

4. Background (Family History, Relationships and Upbringing)—Is there anything about her past or upbringing that might contribute to her problems? Have her parents been contributive factors either because of a present form of interference, or because of a specific style of child-raising and a past of poor family dynamics that were practiced as she grew up? Does she have personal, damaging baggage that affects her everyday life (we all do)? Has she experienced personal life traumas or events that might cause her to commit actions outside of normal expectations? Does she demonstrate an inability to trust or relate to others?

Here are some thoughts about Dr. Crabb's Four Circles that might assist the disciple investor in understanding the significance of how each circle functions as a diagnostic tool. Firstly, I believe that the most enlightening thing to pursue (or circle to explore) would be to approach the circle addressing *feelings*. The reason for this approach, as I have found, lies in the reality that people will talk more easily and express themselves more vibrantly if the conversation focuses more on feelings than thinking. Also, people are often quick to lie about their behavior if shame, failure, or guilt is involved so it is best not to focus initially on behavior. Further, people don't respond as well to the "thinking" category—either they don't know what they actually do think or cannot put their thinking into words. Most people are much better at expressing their emotions than their thoughts. As a matter of fact, their real thinking often flows from their emotions. It is not that they cannot think or explain, but that they often are not inclined to think. People are often much more in touch with their emotions than their thoughts, whatever the issue or matter might be.

Secondly, I have discovered that I can uncover much about a person's real attitudes, needs, and concerns when I delve into past life experiences, i.e., the fourth circle. People like to talk about themselves and almost always appreciate it when someone wants to hear about their experiences. If, as a physician of the soul and a practitioner of spiritual diagnostics, I focus on a person's past experiences, family upbringing, formative years, as well as his past trials, joys, victories, and accomplishments (i.e., the many developmental forces that shaped him while growing up), I find that the individual will unveil further and deeper insights into his life, thinking, needs, hopes, and dreams. Initially, I thought that the "background" circle appeared more Freudian in its basis and origins, but eventually I realized that it was a profitable means to truly discover what lies within the potential disciple. Therefore, contrary to the usual approach I would normally pursue (i.e., trying to discover how people think and behave or operate), I actually make inquiry regarding feelings and personal experiences. Using this approach usually allows me to eventually discover an individual's thoughts and practices.

Diagnostic Tool: The Engle Scale of Evangelism

In the early years of Reformed Theological Seminary Charlotte, I had the privilege of working with Dr. Will Norton, former missionary, missiologist, professor, seminary president, and three-time retiree from ministry! At the time I didn't realize that this aging and experienced educator was the co-author, along with Dr. James F. Engle, of a book I had read some years previously while in seminary, *What's Gone Wrong with the Harvest?* But it didn't take long to recognize that this eighty year old gentleman was all about proclaiming Christ to the world. His passion was The Great Commission! In their book, Drs. Norton and Engle build a case that the problem with the church today in getting the gospel message out to the world essentially lies in the failure to communicate—this failure involves the inability for believers and the church to understand their audience and how to adapt the message to the intended audience.

Probably the most profitable (and popular) concept derived from *What's Gone Wrong with the Harvest?* is the presentation of Dr. Engle's diagnosis of the audience (or receptors), known now as "The Engle Scale." The Engle Scale (which has since been revised and reworked by many) was profound in that it provided the aspiring evangelist with a grid to help understand the starting point from which the listener was coming. According to the scale, evangelists or believers need to delve into (or analyze) the spiritual background of the person to whom they are speaking. What does the individual already comprehend about God and the gospel? What specifics does this person understand or what knowledge is lacking? The Engle Scale helps believers understand the starting point of their audience and adapt their presentation of the gospel accordingly. At the very least, the scale provides a means for sensitivity in diagnosis of the spiritual awareness of a given individual. I believe it continues to be a helpful chart in the disciple investing and "soul diagnosis" process. Below is the Engle Scale in its simplest form.

The Engle Scale

- -10 Awareness of the supernatural
- -9 No effective knowledge of Christianity
- -8 Initial awareness of Christianity
- -7 Interest in Christianity
- -6 Awareness of basic facts of the gospel
- -5 Grasp of implications of the gospel
- -4 Positive attitude to the gospel
- -3 Awareness of personal need
- -2 Challenge and decision to act
- -1 Repentance and faith
- 0 A disciple is born
- +1 Evaluation of decision
- +2 Initiation into the church

+3	Becomes part of the process of making other disciples
+4	Growth in understanding of the faith
+5	Growth in Christian character
+6	Discovery and use of gifts
+7	Christian life-style
+8	Stewardship of resources
+9	Prayer
+10	Openness to others/Effective sharing of faith and life[3]

One does not need to memorize the Engle Scale to find it useful. Eventually, as a disciple investor works with people and develops a personal mentality of "spiritual diagnosis," he will think naturally in these categories whether using Engle's exact terms or not. Nevertheless, as a framework for ministry, The Engle Scale is quite helpful.

The Need for Diagnosis

I have often told my seminary students that I have literally stood by and watched someone approach a lawyer friend of mine (and even my late father) when they discovered that their profession was law and ask, "Do you have a moment to give me some free legal advice?" I have seen people approach a doctor during "off hours" and ask him for a free, off-the-record medical opinion. Very rarely, however, have I ever had an individual approach me or know of one approaching some other minister with this thought or statement, "Rod, I know you're a minister; lately I have been having some real struggles in my soul or questions about my faith or uncertainty about my eternal destiny. Would you please give me some time and attention so that I can gain strength and answers and become a healthier Christian?" Surprisingly, or maybe not so surprisingly, people, including genuine Christians or active church members, do not open themselves up to the "qualified spiritual professionals" of what was once known as the highest of the three top respected professions. But, they might open up to you, if you are a concerned, approachable friend with an open heart and ear. The personal problems of life are there, they are real and must be faced.

3. Adapted from *What's Gone Wrong with the Harvest?* By James F. Engel and Wilbert Norton.

And you can be a part of the diagnostic process with them simply by caring and listening. If indeed you aspire to disciple others and invest in their lives, you can function, in some ways, as a member of the body of Christ who looks out for and speaks into the heart needs of others. I imagine that ordinary members of the body of Christ can fulfill the ministry of diagnosing other believer's needs as well as the professionals, although they might need some help with the deeper questions and answers.

God the Great Counselor in Spiritual Diagnosis

There is one who can answer the deeper questions and answers if we are seeking for and looking to him. I am reminded of a story told by the professor of RTS Charlotte mentioned above, Dr. Will Norton. Most of his stories were memorable! During the early days of World War II, Dr. Norton and his wife, Coleen, served as missionaries in the Congo. While there, they had three children, one of whom died. Their life was not easy to say the least. They served faithfully until the end of the war. At this point, Dr. Norton believed it was time for the family to return to the States. They travelled to the coast where they hoped to catch a boat home to recover from their taxing mission to Africa. Dr. Norton approached an official at the American embassy entreating him to allow his family to take the next ship heading home. Although the family had hoped to go immediately, with the alternative being to stay in Africa indefinitely while waiting for the next ship, Dr. Norton's appeals were rejected. The official stated that *everyone* wanted to return home to America and he demanded to know who Dr. Norton was that he should receive any preferential treatment. Dr. Norton was both shocked and saddened.

As I listened to him tell this story for the first time in 1996, I vividly recall his profound statement, "Here I was in one of the most devastating, difficult, stressful, and unsolvable situations I could ever imagine—seemingly hopeless and there was *no counselor* around anywhere!" He concluded, "It was just me and God. And that's how we got through!" And God did provide for this simple, trusting man of God, seeing him and his family through the night at a Salvation Army station up the road, sleeping with his wife and children on the floor. And eventually, they were able to get home. What a personal counselor! What a great God! Ultimately, the best solutions for our life problems begin and end with the living God, who cares for us and intervenes. He knows our problems; he has the solutions.

He has spoken, he is present, he will act, let us listen to and trust him. He will counsel us in our time of need!

Personal Application

Spiritual diagnosis provides insight into people's lives and the problems they face. How they feel and behave is inevitably caused by their flawed thinking. We all have flaws in our thinking. Hence, when we operate as counselors, we should strive to be "Bible teachers" who explain the tenets and principles of Scripture as they apply to life's challenges and expectations. We want to help people with their heart problems, which requires that we address the three domains of the heart as we offer our advice and counsel. We want people to "*believe* the right thing; *love* the right way; *do* the right thing." We want them to hear and respond to God's word, embrace his wisdom with a reverent and cherishing spirit and to desire to walk in God's will and ways.

These prescriptions are not moralism. They are wholehearted responses to following Christ as Lord through the power of the Holy Spirit. Listening to the grand physician usually requires humble repentance. When our doctor tells us what is wrong with our health and then prescribes an antidote or solution, we are considered responsive patients when we take his advice to heart seriously and then go home and begin new habits. Such a response is what the disciple investor hopes for in the counselee: full submission to God's revealed will, attended by passion and practice and led by his Spirit. God's law is our guide; Christ-likeness is our hope. Perfection is our model; maturity is our goal.

Dealing with Repentance: Christ Changing Lives!

The doctrine of repentance is crucial to understanding the normal Christian life. It must be a part of our daily walk with Christ. Therefore, as direct and revealing as the question might be, it never hurts for the inquiring disciple investor to ask, "Is there anything in your life about which you should repent?" And, "Are you willing to repent of the specific sin with which you are struggling?" The late Dr. Jack Miller of Westminster Theological Seminary and New Life Church of Philadelphia, wrote a classic text called *Repentance and 20th Century Man* (now simply entitled *Repentance* and revised a bit by his wife, Rose). Dr. Miller explains that repentance is a way of life for the serious follower of Christ. This small and simple volume is an excellent introduction to and treatment of the subject of repentance and would be an excellent guide for studying the topic with another person. Repentance is a way of life for the serious believer in Christ.

Beware of Attachment and Dependency

One common problem in the disciple investing relationship is the potential scenario in which a new believer depends too much upon the counsel, wisdom, or influence of the disciple investor. In particular, this problem could rear its ugly head within an exclusive one-on-one discipling context. This danger is one reason why I believe that the Apostle Paul did not overtly espouse one-on-one discipleship in spite of what some ministries propose. This is not to say that we should not do one-on-one disciple investing; rather, we should focus on helping any new believers in whatever way possible, while maintaining a philosophy that we are indeed only "investing" in their lives, not becoming the only conduit that helps them grow in Christ. I discovered in ministry, whether church or campus, that others might build an undue attachment to me based on the nature of a consistent relationship, or because I was a high-profile leader with not only spiritual interest in others but a willingness to care, meet, and listen.

College students would appear to be a more dangerous "market" for attachment and dependency, but I found there was greater danger in the context of the church rather than the campus. In reality, I did not have any one-on-one ministries with women in the local church setting, but the dependency toward my position as senior pastor placed me in some awkward spots in which single or single-again females leaned too strongly on me emotionally. However, I was able to practice objective counseling with a measure of detachment without fostering or encouraging dependence. You might be very different in your method of operating. Everyone needs to know their limits with friendships and discipling relationships with both the same and opposite sex. We must also always remember the adage that I once heard from the late Dr. Frank Kik, former professor of Practical Theology at RTS Charlotte. Speaking to fledgling ministers who were still in seminary, he would always remind them, saying, "You're not going to save the world." When we realize that it is the Lord, and not us as disciple investors, who changes people and grows them up into Christ-likeness, we begin to recognize that we are only vessels that the Lord uses in the process of sanctification. Disciples of Christ are ultimately being discipled by Christ and they need to find their dependence upon him and be attached to him, the living vine, in order to live and face each new day.

Access-Advice-Application-Accountability

Here is a simple formula useful for describing the disciple investing process: build a genuine relationship that provides access to the disciple's life. Access includes the ability to ask appropriate diagnostic questions about the individual's spiritual growth and well-being. Once the disciple opens up about his life and you have built a trust relationship, you can give advice (or prescription/salve) based upon Scripture. Based upon this advice, the disciple can implement this action (or apply the advice) in order to deal with areas of growth or weakness. Then in the realm of accountability, you as disciple investor can appraise and evaluate the implementation in the context of an ongoing relationship (follow-up). Progress or struggle can be observed, discussed, and evaluated.

The Possibility of Professional Help

I believe that the Scriptures are wholly adequate to solve the heart and soul problems of any man or woman of any age, time, or culture. The gospel is powerful and transformative. Christ is not a concept but a person, the very son of God. Meeting him changes everything about a person. The primary goal of disciple investing is to help a person know Christ better and become like Christ more and more. Part of the disciple investing process, as mentioned earlier, includes helping believers overcome and deal with their personal sins, problems, and baggage.

However, sometimes the extent of these problems is so deep that weekly or regular meetings are too difficult to sustain. Sometimes the combination of multiplied deep problems is so extensive that you as a disciple investor may begin to feel that the great weight of the burdens is too heavy for you to bear. Sometimes people become a drain upon the disciple investor primarily because they do not respond to the prescription of Scripture or the wisdom given. These people take but do not move forward. Many years ago, I heard Dr. Tim Keller say that he had experienced such people and he described them as "black-hole" persons. Black-hole is an apt description and anyone who has ever worked with such people will fully understand this concept. You, the disciple maker, pour time, life, advice, and help into the other person's soul. And then you look down into that soul and the progress that you hope it will make, and all you see is a black hole—there is nothing visible in existence as a result of your efforts.

Eventually, the wise disciple investor will realize that this person needs someone else's help. As difficult as it might be to admit, you need to recognize your own limits and send the individual to someone else, most probably a professional. A local pastor who loves or specializes in counseling from a biblical standpoint or a Christian counselor who is biblically grounded are excellent avenues for regular support in the life of this individual. When unresponsive disciples realize that they will be (potentially) paying for biblical advice, they might take the sound counsel they are receiving more seriously and respond accordingly. This should be your hope and prayer as a disciple investor and the primary reason for utilizing a professional resource, whether a Christian counselor or local pastor.

Diagnosing Spiritual Background

Religious Background

One of the most insightful and intriguing points of entry into a person's life is discovering the person's church or denominational background, if any. You wish to know: has she ever had a church? Is she presently churched or unchurched? If she is Protestant, to what denomination does her church belong or with what church does she see herself affiliating? If she does not fully understand the terms or traditions, would she consider her church fundamentalist (militant or not), conservative, mainline, and/or liberal? If disciples claim to be of the Roman Catholic Church, try to discover if they are traditional, conservative, charismatic, progressive, or liberal. If Jewish, are they from an Orthodox, Conservative, Reformed, or liberal tradition? Are they Unitarian or universalist in background? Possibly, they might claim to be Pagan—are they atheistic or agnostic? With most of these traditions, it is reasonable to ask people what their church or denomination's view of the Bible is and how the Bible impacts their church and denomination (they may know little about these nuances). It would also be reasonable to ask about any church/religious retreats or conferences they may have attended. Even if they have rarely been involved in a local church or congregation, they may have been invited to a special church event and could tell you a lot about it. This discussion could open a lot of other doors for insightful conversation.

Beliefs of Church

In the diagnostic process, this is where the fun begins. There is nothing more enjoyable or insightful than asking people about their church's teachings. Most people only have a vague idea about what their home church believes. However, in asking these questions, the disciple investor is enabled to enter a very accessible door into the individual's own beliefs and convictions (or lack thereof). The disciple investor, as one who diagnoses, is able to discover if the disciple has any theological depth in his understanding or whether he can articulate what he does believe. This articulation comes more easily since the conversation revolves around the church; even if an individual must guess about the church's doctrine, his answers allow the listener to discern if he has any comprehension of the basic and deeper truths of Scripture. Opinions of the church, whether positive or negative, are invaluable in assessing how the individual responds to spiritual authority and teaching, or any spiritual guidance that the disciple investor might provide. True feelings about church, ministry, and spiritual guidance often come out in this frank and open context of conversation.

View of Pastor

Asking the aspiring disciple to describe his experience with pastors from the past provides an open forum towards discussion about spiritual matters. The disciple investor should discover whether the person has had positive experiences with previous pastors. If the experiences have been negative, ask the individual to describe them. On the other hand, was there a pastor who made a positive impact in the person's life or among any of his family members? What role has this positive influence had? Let him explain what he thinks the role of the pastor should be in the local church. Is there any popular pastor, preacher (local or not), or televangelist that he likes, acknowledges (or dislikes)? Find out why he gravitates toward or avoids this spiritual leader. A disciple investor can discover plenty of spiritual insight with answers to those questions.

Preaching Emphasis: if an individual has had some past exposure to preaching of any type, in any context, this experience can also provide a barometer of spiritual awareness and knowledge. Most people don't remember the exact content of a given sermon but they can give opinions about what they sense might be the tenor or emphasis of a preaching style or method. Answers to a simple question such as, "What type of sermons did your pastor preach?" can tell the disciple investor volumes about the ministry perspective under which the disciple sat. Other questions related to preaching might be, "Did your pastor preach from the Bible (as opposed to storytelling, *Readers Digest* quotes, or political issues)?" "Did your pastor read the Bible and then talk about what the Bible said?" "Did your pastor read from the Bible and then talk about something entirely different?" "Is there some memorable sermon that you recall? If so, what was it about?" These are great leading questions for further discussion.

Good and Bad Experiences

Although related to the four topics above, this category of experiences is a little more open-ended and comprehensive. Even people outside the church can have good or bad encounters with groups or individuals who are associated with faith of some kind. The disciple investor should discern whether the person has ever had any type of personal religious experience.[4] Has he ever had a positive encounter with any Christian individual, church, or ministry group? Why was the experience positive and did he take away anything positive from this encounter? Has he been impacted adversely by some Christian group or individual? (Permit him to speak at length without defending the perpetrators—in this manner, a disciple investor can learn a lot, and build some trust and sympathy.) It is very positive to hear out complaints or painful experiences as this helps the speaker unload some "religious baggage" and also allows the listener to discern the speaker's level of receptivity to possible help in the future. What does the disciple think would make the church a better place? (This is a very enlightening question.)

---

4. Listen closely for possible descriptions of phony mysticism or false religious experiences.

Ministry Involvement

The disciple investor should also learn whether the individual has served the church or the Lord in any manner. It is entirely possible that the person has not only been involved in a local church or some sort of parachurch ministry, but has also served in some way, large or small. The disciple investor ought to discover the nature of this experience to ascertain whether or not the disciple has positive feelings toward doing ministry, or has used ministry gifts of some type. He can also discern the presence of potential leadership that may need to be utilized or developed. Can the disciple lead? Has he led any ministry? What exactly has he done in ministry? Can he work with a team—is he a team player? Does he seek the glory of God and the good of the ministry above his own glory, status, or achievement? Is he humble? Is he reliant upon the Lord, trusting him to do his work through him? What is his attitude toward authority? Can he submit to authority when necessary? Does he understand the differences between working in a local church setting and working in a parachurch ministry setting? Does he have particular abilities and giftedness working with specific age groups? Where does he struggle with the realities of ministry? Will he need much oversight, guidance, mentoring, training, or hand-holding?

7

Method and Models of Discipleship

(Disciple Investing)

THE SIMPLE DEFINITION OF disciple investing, as mentioned earlier, would be stated thusly: "Disciple investing is the development of true, committed, and dedicated followers (or learners) of Jesus."

My more comprehensive definition of a disciple of Christ, as given in chapter 1, would be . . .

> A Christian disciple is one who by God's grace has become a learner, a lover, and a follower of Jesus Christ. This follower is one who walks by faith in relationship with the risen Christ, and whose mind, emotions, and will are submitted to and changed by Christ's word and his Spirit, so that the disciple obediently loves the triune God more and more and is becoming conformed to Christ's likeness more and more and serving more and more in his body, the church. The process of discipleship occurs in the community of Christ's church and involves multiple and various avenues of influence—people, home life, activities, personal experience, ministries outside of the church—in such a way that Jesus Christ uses "all of life" to sovereignly work in his disciple's life in order to glorify his heavenly Father.

I believe that ultimately, today as always, Christ is still choosing, calling, and discipling his followers. Jesus wants us to know him, become more like him, and to be involved in pointing others to him. But how does he disciple us today? I believe the obvious answer is that Jesus uses his people and his church as the avenue to start, to continue, and to persevere through the process of disciple investing in order that every follower may become a mature disciple of Jesus.

But, as any experienced believer in Christ knows, there are a variety of approaches or methods used in the disciple investing process. A study of church history would demonstrate that there have been a multitude of methods used to help others become better disciples of Jesus, from house churches, mystical asceticism (and escapes from reality), a focus upon and use of the spiritual disciplines, pietistic emphases on heartfelt religion, liturgical worship, Bible-based reformation, Sunday School programs, revivalism, an emphasis on the social gospel, the Christian school movement, and youth ministry to name a few. I would like to present a few major categories of disciple investing in an attempt to understand their methods, their strengths, and their weaknesses.

Methods and Models of Disciple Investing

Personal Discipleship

Personal discipleship, or personal disciple investing, focuses upon the individual as a primary means of helping others follow Christ fully. Personal discipleship is the process of learning to follow Christ through another individual or other individuals, normally in a relational context. The onus is upon the individual being discipled and the individual discipling. Personal discipleship can be done apart from a system, program, or ministry. I once contacted a young man I had known in an earlier church setting in order to meet with him and help him understand how to grow as a Christian (he may or may not have been a Christian at the time). We did not attend the same church and as a matter of fact, I don't think he attended any church at the time. But I spent an hour or so each week during the summer with him discussing his life and the life that Christ would have us live. There was no organization involved in any way, church or parachurch. This structure probably describes "personal" disciple investing in its most blatant form. Neither of us answered to or was held accountable by anyone but the Lord. Nevertheless, I would appraise the time as a helpful one, although the young man might not have. I'm not sure if or how he sensed any benefit to the personal time and attention I gave him, but I do know that he had to deal with some moral issues and a lack of integrity in his own life.

System Discipleship

System discipleship is the process of learning to follow Christ through the holistic influence of an organization, whether in and through a church or some other type of ministry context. The system includes individuals, but there is a strong organizational or systematic ethos pervading both the group and the individuals. The involvement of people in systematic discipleship includes the possibility of strong, personal one-on-one meetings, but in general the system tends to lean on a programmatic format revolving around the purposes and mission of the organization. The system (or ministry) itself defines the method and means of discipleship and it is almost always designed to benefit the organization that has designed, sponsored, or endorsed it. Hence, the system includes a strong organizational or systematic ethos, one that is well-defined and explained through the vision casting process.

This type of discipleship includes high expectations and demands of its followers, and often these expectations are put in very accessible written form (a quality control manual of sorts). If followers do not initially understand the expectations and demands, the organization will teach these to them in either a group or one-on-one context. Sometimes this context is considered to be part of the training of a disciple (or participant). Conformity is an intrinsic value in system discipleship and usually includes the pressure of the group or system.

System discipleship as a method is often reflected in style by parachurch ministries, nevertheless, denominations and church traditions are not immune to it. In historic Presbyterianism and the Reformed tradition, the "system" was maintained by starting early, i.e., catechizing children at a young age. Then, the "Communicants Class" would confirm the acceptance of belief necessary for membership in the church (usually at age twelve). If a church used a comprehensive denominational educational curriculum (as opposed to a free choice curriculum), the system would continue to hope for conformity to previously taught and confirmed belief systems. I personally would not use the term "disciple investing" for this because I think if wholeheartedly embraced by the disciple, it has the potential to become too oppressive. Systems do invest in people's lives, but they can become too demanding and controlling with a passion to recruit people who will invest in it.

An Exercise: Personal versus System Discipleship

1. Name three (or more) people who have made a significant spiritual impact on your life. Of these people, pick three and answer the following questions:

    A. What was your relationship to this person?

    B. What did each person teach you about the Christian life?

    C. What was each person's strength?

    D. What was each person's weakness?

    E. Optional Question: Did this happen in your church? If not, where did it happen?

2. Name two (or more) systems that have made a significant impact on your spiritual life[1] or walk with the Lord. Choose two systems and answer these questions:

    A. What did each system teach you about the Christian life?

    B. What was each system's strength?

    C. What was each system's weakness?

    D. What was your relationship to this system? (position/time)

Discussion Question: Compare and contrast the benefits of both personal and system discipleship.

At-Large Discipleship ("All of Life" Discipleship)

At-Large Discipleship asks the question, "What else has changed your life in such a way that you have become more Christ-like?" The premise of at-large disciple investing is that when followers of Christ sit under the variety of Christian influences that intersect with their lives, they are changed or impacted by those respective ministries. Some of the at-large influences in a person's life might be Christian or church events, sermons, lectures, camps, retreats and conferences, trials sent by God, church activities and outings,

---

1. I might add that, as mentioned earlier, the most formative systems in my early Christian development were: 1) Southern Baptist Convention local church; 2) The Navigators, a campus ministry; 3) Cru (Campus Crusade for Christ).

mission trips, summer projects, books and articles (with their respective authors), Christian blogs and websites, Christian celebrities and personalities, personal studies, ministry responsibilities, personal disciplines, Christian concerts or choir/band ensembles, television and radio evangelists and preachers, drama teams, Christian comedians, mimes, sports teams and ministries, mercy ministries and outreaches, etc. You the reader might be able to add some other "at-large" influences that have drawn you closer to Christ or Christ-likeness.

Organic Discipleship

Organic disciple investing would be defined as a focus on the spiritual growth of the individual in whom ministry occurs through the corporate influence of the community of believers. Organic disciple investing is derived from the impact of that community and its corporate activities (comprehensive body-life) upon the participants (disciples). Disciple investing occurs as a part of everyday living together in, and affiliation with, a community of believers. Spiritual growth (as well as possible conversion to Christ) is a natural consequence of an environment of intentional gospel-focused and Christ-centered endeavors through the Holy Spirit. The organic method has the appearance of being a living, moving, thriving organism which appeals to onlookers and even participants. The group culture of "organism" on the surface appears much more alive than the structure of a ministry characterized by organization. A structured organization often seems to exemplify a loss of the apparent vitality of a living, vital organism (though that is not always the case).

Strengths of the organic disciple investing method would be, firstly, the interdependent nature of the community of believers, i.e., the beauty of Christ's people, his body, living together in unity and reliance upon one another. Organic disciple investing is relational in nature, another appeal of the method. Because of the relational ethos, growth in Christ appears to be more natural and unforced, as opposed to people being pushed into programs, strategies, and planned structures. The absence of a top-down or authoritative person or program is seen as a blessing. The more recent rise of collegial leadership in the local church and among other organizations reflects something of the philosophy of organic group movement, supporting parity in leadership as well as team work among all of its members. Organic disciple investing is also pastoral in nature since individual needs prevail in this approach. Personal spiritual growth is predicated and dependent upon the use of the means of grace instead of being driven by a ministry's goals or desire for growth or expansion. Possibly its greatest strength is the beauty of full reliance on the role of the Holy Spirit to affect change in the lives of disciples.

Weaknesses of organic disciple investing most certainly flow out of its strengths. At times, because ministry appears to "go with the flow," the organic method seems directionless. Undefined ministry just happens. One former college student who was involved with a ministry known for its organic nature told me, "They don't seem to do any evangelism." And upon further reflection, he stated, "And they don't seem to do any discipleship either." Passivity and non-involvement of members and participants can become the ethos of the group. The organic method of disciple investing often needs more structure, design, and particularly intentionality.

Often it is difficult to evaluate progress. How do you measure individual or group growth? Usually, standards of measurement return to the *numbers game*—how many people are attending, how many small groups are occurring, and how many people are showing up to the various activities and ministries. Proponents sometimes refer to Jesus's discipleship as appearing very organic, but a closer study of his methods reveals that he had plans, goals, aspirations, and a training regimen of sorts. The organic method of disciple investing, which I do espouse in many ways and for many reasons, sometimes reminds me of the iconic 1950s American horror movie *The Blob*, starring the late Steve McQueen. The movie was advertised as "Indescribable, indestructible, nothing can stop it!" The blob started small and gradually grew, swallowing up anything that stood in its way, much like a living, growing organism. Whatever lay in its path became a part of the blob. Organic disciple investing sometimes seems like that—it grows indiscriminately, taking members upon itself, usually in a healthy manner, but without distinguishing or focusing upon the individuals. Yet change is occurring among the group as well as among its members and oftentimes, very positive things are happening. (Okay, maybe that *is* unlike the blob).

Programmatic Discipleship

Programmatic disciple investing is defined as a focus on the spiritual growth of the individual whereas the goal of the ministry is attained through a planned and/or structured (programmatic) method of learning and experience. Programs come in all shapes and sizes, beginning with the most commonly acknowledged program, Sunday School (which originated in 1780 as literacy training for chimney sweeps and street waifs in London and yes, it was criticized by the churches of that day). Programs are also espoused by parachurch ministry plans, such as the Navigators' *Colossians 2:7 Series* or Cru's *Ten Transferable Steps*, to Awana Club and Pioneer Club children's programs. Other adult-oriented programs would include the very popular *Experiencing God* series by Henry Blackerby and Serge Ministry's mentoring plan known as *Sonship*. I imagine that the list of discipleship programs is almost endless, depending on the denomination, the parachurch ministry, the sponsoring local church, and the independent publisher.

Programmatic discipleship often gets criticized and there are some legitimate reasons for hesitating to implement a program in a church or ministry. The program assumes that its material and design is of utmost priority and therefore takes precedence over specific individual needs. However, this method of disciple investing does have some notable strong points. Although the subject matter (or goals of the program) does take priority over the learner, the ability to intently study a given subject in a consistent manner is a real strength. If indeed the subject matter is presented with high quality, there is an assurance (or assumption) that the students or recipients will have the opportunity to grasp the truth of the matter. Programs also are capable of presenting measurable goals to the participants and may provide a sense of potential accomplishment of those goals. Another positive strength is that programmatic disciple investing provides a very structured and controlled environment for learning. Additionally, the program is usually achievable and progress not only is measurable but can provide encouragement to the disciple upon completion. Programs usually include short-term expectations that assist the participants in accomplishing either the assigned task or the focus of study in the program.

However, programmatic disciple investing includes some glaring weaknesses. It has the potential to be task-oriented rather than people-oriented. The program often supersedes people: the purpose is either the accomplishment of the task or the fulfillment of the requirements. Both are more important than the needs of the participants. People are involved, but the program is predominant. This approach can come across as cold or harsh. Programmatic disciple investing is very often inflexible in its structure. Deviation is usually not allowed. Because the focus is upon going through, or fulfilling the requirements of the program, and becomes task-oriented, it may miss the heart. Task fulfillment might be celebrated above needed changes, and heart transformation might not occur at all. Even when the program is completed, disciples need to realize that their discipleship is incomplete; they are a work in progress. On the other hand, disciples might go through the program, gain a sense of completion, and with that sense determine that they can "ease up" on their efforts of following Christ or gain a false sense of pride from their accomplishments or newfound statuses in the program. Neither is a positive result of programmatic disciple investing, even though programs can assuredly be positive in their impact.

Military Discipleship

Military disciple investing requires a high demand or regimented model of performance, including high expectations and strict submission and obedience throughout the prescribed process. This emphasis toward spiritual growth in the individual only occurs through fulfilling well laid out or explained methods that contain high demands. In these groups/churches one can see the tendency toward cult-like practices. In cult-like settings the emphasis becomes quite controlling and can include what is known as extreme shepherding. (This often happens in campus ministries where college students are naïve, malleable, and compliant; however, local churches can also build a similar culture.) Christians who pursue or are recruited for this type of disciple investing are either viewed as "the marines of the faith" or at least feel like they have joined the Christian edition of the marines. These groups or ministries strive to be the best possible followers of Christ and that goal can only be measured by the accomplishment of tasks or explicit requirements given to the participating disciples. Their leaders often express the fact that they are trying to produce the "cream of the crop" in Christian faith, knowledge, and service. Philosophically, results and accomplishments are the ordinary means of evaluating one's progress toward the goal of "Christ-likeness."

Positive attributes of military disciple making are considerable. First of all, those who promote this type of discipleship justify it by declaring that Jesus had (or has) high demands for his disciples. He calls them to deny themselves, take up their crosses daily, and to follow him. Luke 9 contains a compact passage that demonstrates Jesus's demands on his followers:

METHOD AND MODELS OF DISCIPLESHIP

> ²³And he said to all, "If anyone would come after me, let him deny himself and take up his cross daily and follow me. ²⁴ For whoever would save his life will lose it, but whoever loses his life for my sake will save it. ²⁵ For what does it profit a man if he gains the whole world and loses or forfeits himself? ²⁶ For whoever is ashamed of me and of my words, of him will the Son of Man be ashamed when he comes in his glory and the glory of the Father and of the holy angels."[2]

He speaks similarly in Luke 14,

> "If anyone comes to me and does not hate his own father and mother and wife and children and brothers and sisters, yes, and even his own life, he cannot be my disciple. ²⁷Whoever does not bear his own cross and come after me cannot be my disciple."[3]

Since much of the Christianity practiced today is nominal, insipid, and reflects an attitude of words without passion or action, one could understand the desire and motives behind the military model. Some obvious strengths are that military disciple making involves high-demand, high-activity service, and along with high expectations, also high performance. High submission might be a strength but that quality could also be an inherent weakness.

Weaknesses of the military model are stark. It is a model of disciple making that is short on relationships. One doesn't create Christian marines through warm fuzzies, hugs, positivity, or feel-good talks. Relationships are indeed involved and in some contexts, are truly driven by caring ministry. However, the nature of creating high-response and high-demand involvement of the disciple in this context and reaching the ministry's goals often causes the relationship to become a periphery issue. The military disciple making framework (or program) and its expectations are prioritized over people and relationships. Manipulation occurs at lower levels because the pressure is on the leadership (upper tier) to produce mature followers who will become future leaders and recruit others. The leaders may also sink into the sad behavior pattern of motivation by guilt. I know, I've been there!

Another great weakness of this model is that it provides less flexibility in matters of Christian freedom and growth. Military disciple making resembles the programmatic model in this regard. The disciple must conform to the program and respond appropriately or suffer the

2. Luke 9: 23–26.
3. Luke 14: 26–27.

consequences—possible rebuke/dismissal from the group, or removal from potential future leadership roles). Because the military model is so very high-demand, accomplishments by the aspiring disciples are less achievable. Some will drop out of the ministry, often being castigated (at least by implication) as lesser followers of Christ. The weak or non-cooperative may be jettisoned out of the group or the leadership pipeline, leaving deep scars on those who don't measure up to the military standards. On the other hand, because the emphasis in this model is upon achievement and accomplishment, the disciples (and their leaders) may become self-reliant. A spirit of self-effort and dependence upon personal ability may cause the individual (as well as the group) to underestimate the need for the Holy Spirit in both sanctification and service. Self-reliance and the flesh, rather than humility and faith, may reign in this model.

The Three Avenues of Ministry and Disciple Investing

As one considers philosophies of ministry, whether inside or out of the local church, the inevitable conclusion is that three obvious avenues of ministry and disciple investing exist: one-on-one ministry, small group ministry, and large group ministry.

One-on-One (Individual Disciple Investing)

One-on-one ministry would consist of the following:

A. Counseling

B. Visitation and follow-up

C. Hanging out with another person

D. Personal and possible relational evangelism

E. Personal disciple investing

F. Leadership (or disciple investing) training

G. Appointments

   1. Unbelievers and the unchurched
   2. New ministry/church contacts and visitors
   3. Return contacts or visitors

4. Follow-up of any person in contact with the ministry or those involved in/with the ministry
   5. Potential/future leaders
   6. Rising leaders
   7. Present leaders
H. Leadership development/planning/strategy
I. Teaching, encouraging, rebuking, and exhortation
J. Relationship building (fun and fellowship)
K. Personal ministry to the needy (widows, sick, the elderly, orphans, the disadvantaged, or disenfranchised)

Small Group Ministry
(three to fifteen individuals)

These are examples of small group ministry:

A. Bible studies for spiritual growth
B. Bible studies designed for evangelism
C. Session/Consistory/Advisory/Core group (church or ministry leaders) training, prayer, planning
D. Small group leader training
E. Sunday school classes (if fewer than twelve-fifteen)
F. Fellowship meals (around the tables and in homes)
G. Choir
H. Most committees
I. Teacher training (for a particular age group or department)
J. Session (elders) and Diaconate (deacons), i.e., stated or regularly scheduled monthly or bi-monthly meetings
K. After church meals or coffee with invited guests
L. Leadership development/training/planning/strategy
M. Ministry-focused projects
N. Mission groups/committee (local and international)

Large Group Meetings (usually more than twelve to fifteen people gathered together)

Large Group Meetings in ministry could be as follows:

A. Worship service/celebration: Although the current culture emphasizes the individual, the worship of God is at its best when it is experienced in a corporate setting, particularly in the local church. Worship includes praying together, giving unto the Lord as a gathered group of believers, hearing the preached word together, praising God in song, and participating in corporately administered sacraments (not privately, or without guarding the communion table; private communion may be appropriate in a small group service in a home or hospital for those infirmed and homebound, using elders to shepherd the process). Whether emphasizing contemplation or celebration in worship, using a structured liturgy, or allowing guided spontaneity, gathering as a large group to seek and honor the Lord impacts and transforms followers of Christ.

B. Church-wide activities: Gathering together to enjoy one another in Christian fellowship is imperative in the life of a church and its believers. Informal or planned large group gatherings allow for relaxed communion with other believers and encourages them to experience the diversity of fellowship that exists in the body of Christ. These meetings can be gatherings for dinners, cookouts, ministry, picnics, trips, outings, camping or retreats, anything that might include people of all ages, as well as any activity suitable for interaction together. The depth of fellowship and interaction occurring in a casual large group setting can be powerfully used by the Lord to bring unity to and greater intimacy among believers.

C. Special services or programs: Oftentimes the church or ministry will sponsor planned services to unite the followers in service, mission, and vision. These programs might emphasize international missions or local mission endeavors, or they might focus on Bible teaching (Bible conferences) or a topic relevant to the needs within the church (marriage conferences or financial planning and stewardship). They can also include such common programs as seasonal music, choir presentations or concerts, and the traditional children's ministry known as Vacation Bible School.

METHOD AND MODELS OF DISCIPLESHIP

D. Camps, conferences, retreats: People in the church or any group often fall into patterns of life that become routine or predictable. A camping trip, or church/ministry conference, or retreat can jolt people out of their spiritual haze and stimulate them to more energized walks with Christ and service for his kingdom. Conferences and retreats focusing upon spiritual growth are invaluable in the lives of a congregation. These events also create an ethos of expectation that God is working among his people corporately. They also encourage the body of Christ as a whole to move forward in building the kingdom of God.

E. Work projects sponsored by the entire church or a ministry group: These service projects unite people in their energies and visions. They include such activities as cleaning up a downtrodden area or neighborhood, painting, repairing or restoring a neglected residence (or the church building for that matter), getting involved in various mercy projects such as serving in a soup kitchen, a rescue mission, or building a Habitat for Humanity home. Mercy and service would be the emphasis of the large group gathering.

F. Ministry foci: Gathering people and resources together in order to help those less fortunate in the community would be the desire of this large group endeavor. Good avenues for benevolent work include serving widows or widowers, the elderly, the poor, those going through drug rehabilitation, or involvement with ministries reaching the lost, or ministries that sponsor any of these enterprises.

G. Sunday School classes: In some large churches, Sunday School classes can include up to 200 people. Even in small churches, the adult class can simply be one large group with regular attendance over the common small group quantifier consisting of three to fifteen people. The power and influence of a large group of people gathered around the study of God's Word, if harnessed, can be utilized to change the life and culture of a church. Its momentum can impact growing disciples' lives simply by the sheer volume of committed believers joined in unison to tackle any ministry project or goal.

H. Session and Diaconate together (joint officers' meeting): One potential large group in the local church that should never be overlooked is the combined force of the church's officers. Joint officer (elders, alongside the deacons) meetings, as well as officer retreats, can both set the vision for the church and also provide all types of influence and resources to move forward and change or improve the church ministry ethos and work.

The Three Domains and Disciple Investing: Cognition, Affection, and Volition (Behavior)

When we think of disciple investing, it is very easy to fall into the trap of believing that the key to successful discipleship is the priority of imparting knowledge in order for spiritual growth to occur in others. It is easy to fall into this mentality since the problem of biblical illiteracy in our nation is vast and growing. We most certainly need more knowledge of God's word and his will. However, knowledge alone is not the answer. The entire person, mind, emotion, and will must be impacted and transformed by the gospel. I would like to look at the three learning domains (know/feel/do) and how each impacts the disciple investing process.

Cognitive Discipleship

As mentioned above, this is what we normally think of when we consider the concept of discipleship or disciple making, i.e., we want to fill individuals with all types of knowledge and provide the answers that they will need for living the Christian life in the real world. And indeed, knowledge (the correct knowledge—orthodoxy or biblical thinking) is important and powerful. People need to both know and understand (comprehend) the Lord's ways and his will as based upon his revelation of himself in Scripture, as well as through his redemptive work in the world. Orthodox, Scripture-based knowledge is our starting point but it cannot end there. How do we disseminate knowledge to followers of Christ? Here I have listed some methods for delivering "content" in ministry:

A. Teaching/preaching (didactic/lecture) with follow-up discussion—This approach is probably the "purist" form of cognitive delivery, i.e., the dissemination of a lot of material or information in a short period of time. This method works well as long as the teacher is interesting and minimizes distractions. And of course, Jesus used it, so the reader can't critique this method too harshly!

B. Fill-in-the blank booklets—The individual walks through a book of the Bible or topic using material designed to help the person read one or more passages. The student or reader then answers prescribed "fill-in-the-blank" questions about the topic from the passage. This is a very elementary approach to the Scriptures but still effective for many.

C. Short answer discussion questions—Small groups read a passage of Scripture or discuss a topic of biblical interest and answer questions based on the passage or the topic.

D. Book studies—Participants read a book (a chapter or two at a time) and then discuss the material covered through the use of follow-up questions. This method works very well when desiring to focus on a particular topic. Of course, it does require that the participants read the prescribed material!

E. Video/Audio lessons with discussion questions/groups—A group of believers view or listen to a study or presentation/lecture on most any topic of biblical interest. Then they spend a designated percentage of time in a question-and-answer, open-discussion session. Dr. R. C. Sproul's *Ligonier Ministries* has specialized in this educational and training format for decades (and I highly recommend them).

F. Modified inductive Bible study—A leader selects a manageable portion of Scripture (a paragraph or five to ten verses) and questions the text with a view to both comprehending the word of God and applying it to life. The best means to approach this study is to choose a portion of Scripture (a few chapters, e.g., *The Sermon on the Mount*) or a short book of the Bible (e.g., Philippians or 1 Peter) and divide it into ten to fourteen sections for lesson plans with a goal of walking through the entire portion of Scripture in a verse-by-verse study.

G. Topical studies—A group studies a given topic (e.g., prayer, faithfulness, abortion, worry) with guided/open discussion, including short-answer questions. Topical studies can use a passage of Scripture, a book or a pamphlet on the topic, or a collection of Scriptures that cover the topic.

Question of balance: Consider whether or not your ministry of disciple investing is too cognitive. This consideration causes us to pause as we reflect on this important question: Am I balanced? That is, because you are cognitive-oriented in your personal ministry, do you convey the importance of *feeling* truth or *applying* truth to your disciple(s), or do you simply assume it, or worse yet, ignore those other two domains?

Affective Discipleship

Dealing with a person's feelings or emotions is often our primary method of interacting with a disciple because it is the easiest bridge to build (although I believe that ultimately, knowledge should be our primary focus). People tend to emote rather than think and one's feelings are more easily expressed than logical thought. In John 11:35 (at the death of Lazarus with its attendant grief), we observe that Jesus expressed deep emotions over the needs of people ("Jesus wept"). Also, in Matthew 9:36, we read, "When he saw the crowds, he had compassion for them, because they were harassed and helpless, like sheep without a shepherd." In the Matthew text, the word *compassion* speaks of the actual physical taxation that deep caring prompts in the "feeler." Jesus felt deeply, even physically, for people. So, the feelings and the affective domain are an important facet of the disciple investing process.

How, or in what context, are we able to get others to tell us what they are feeling about themselves, their lives, or their world? Below are some possible answers to this question:

A. Counseling—The late Buck Hatch, one of my former seminary professors, once told me that counseling is simply explaining what the Bible says to another person in a one-on-one setting. I have found that one-on-one ministry naturally spawns counseling. Most people need the attention of another person who is sincerely interested in their lives and well-being. Everyone has problems and although they may not necessarily be, by their very nature, emotional problems, most problems seriously engage the emotions. Feelings are powerful and sharing them, in some ways, is more powerful still. The Bible has answers for the problems that affect emotions, as deeply-seeded as those emotions might be. So, the disciple investor should expect some one-on-one encounters to be "affective" in nature. Confession of struggles, sins, brokenness, and even weeping may occur and out of these emotional expressions, a real desire for change may surface.

B. Shared lives—Personal time with a disciple is invaluable. Disciple investing is best experienced in the context of friendship, when possible.

Personal time includes setting an example of gospel-oriented living and modeling the Christian life. The disciple investing relationship should include the sharing of fun and joy together as well as sorrows and trials. If the old adage, "attitude is more caught than taught" is true (and I believe it is), the sharing of life enhances all sorts of "affective" and emotional disciple investing. Here is the place where lifetime bonds are created and developed. Nothing attaches a person to another individual in loyalty and bonding for life like growing together in Christian friendship, service, and growth.

C. Transparency—Honesty and openness about one's own struggles and personal challenges with another person unites hearts and lives in a way that perfunctory (or programmatic) discipleship never will. People want to be real in the presence of others and they want to be accepted for who they are as well. They need someone before whom they can be personally accountable; as we deal with our own individual sins and failures, we need someone with whom to talk, as well as to discuss our real personal needs. Accountability groups can help in this area and real disciple investing will occur in an open setting such as an accountability group.

D. Dreams/hopes/goals discussion sessions—As people speak about their lives and as the disciple investor speaks into another's life, the topic of the future is almost always relevant. As a matter of fact, rare is the person who does not need to be challenged or questioned about his/her plans, hopes, dreams, short-term, or long-term goals. Sharing dreams (in the proper sense, which means including God as the ultimate priority in one's personal life vision), as well as discussing how to learn to trust God, are very positive interactions to have with another believer. Dreams need to be tethered to reality by understanding the doctrine of the sovereignty of God. But we should also be encouraged as believers to learn to live by faith in a God who is at work. Rather than spinning our wheels or resting satisfied in any number of possible accomplishments, followers of Christ pray to and petition God to do things in their lives that are beyond anything they could ask or imagine. "Now to him who is able to do far more abundantly than all that we ask or think, according to the power at work within us, 21 to him be glory in the church and in Christ Jesus throughout all generations, forever and ever. Amen" (Eph 2:20–21).

E. Prayer groups—Praying together ought to be an emotional experience. In prayer, believers open their hearts, share personal needs and cares, and lift those matters up to the Lord; this action creates and stimulates a spiritual unity of hearts and lives. Praying together for one another and others is a spiritual experience. Jesus promises to be among us as we pray. "For where two or three are gathered in my name, there am I among them" (Matt 18:20). Prayer changes us; thus, the affective domain inevitably will become evident among Christ's followers as they pray.

F. Sacrificial ministry—When one thinks of examples of personal sacrifice, thoughts of the behavioral domain immediately surface. However, viewing or receiving the benefits of another's sacrifice stirs the heart. Evangelist Billy Graham once declared, "No one can take a serious look at the cross and remain unmoved." How can a person contemplate the great sacrifice Christ has made for the sins of his people, the beatings upon his body, even the shedding of blood and his dying under the cruel means of Roman capital punishment, without being personally impacted? And how can people watch a follower of Christ being poured out on behalf of themselves or others, suffering physical pain or personal indignity or loss of any type without being personally moved or shaken? Sacrificial ministry means "being there in crisis or need—weeping with those who weep." Only those who have watched others sacrifice themselves on their behalf can begin to understand the teeming of emotions that it causes. Receiving sacrificial love is one of the greatest promoters of heart "affection" possible.

Question of balance: Consider whether or not your ministry of disciple investing is too affective. This consideration causes us to pause as we reflect on this important question: Am I balanced? That is, because you are relational, do you maintain the importance of conveying knowledge as well as application of knowledge to your disciple, or do you simply assume it or worse yet, ignore those two respective domains?

Volitional/Behavioral Discipleship

Doing Christ-centered and Holy Spirit-motivated ministry always brings a blessing to the soul. Pastor Laurie Vidal, a good friend of mine and the minister who married my wife and me, is also a man who specializes in disciple investing. He once stated, "Obedience brings blessing." He wasn't trying to postulate that if we obey God, he gives us what we want. No, he was proposing that if the follower of Christ seeks to do the will of the Lord, then the Lord, through the presence of the Holy Spirit, will bring joy as well as a spiritual satisfaction to the obedient soul. "Whoever has my commandments and keeps them, he it is who loves me. And he who loves me will be loved by my Father, and I will love him and manifest myself to him" (John 14:21). There is a special intimacy with Christ derived from the life of obedience (i.e., keeping his commandments). *Doing* the Lord's will and living for him, despite any suffering or obstacles one might face, is the life of blessing, assurance, and joy for the Christian. Here are some avenues to pursue in order to build disciples through ministry and activity:

A. Ministry Together—This category is very broad. Ministry together can include doing most anything in Christ's name through a large group, small group, or just two people together (or modeling ministry for another person). Getting people involved in gospel proclamation or service should cause them to learn to depend upon the power of the Holy Spirit. Moving from theory (or theology and/or belief) to application is a tremendous impetus to spiritual growth. Ministry together also creates an environment of life-on-life influence, a wonderful means of disciple investing.

B. Mentoring Activities—Mentoring relationships usually take place in either one-on-one relationships or small group situations. Jesus, of course, mentored and discipled twelve men—that would almost be considered a large group. Certainly, he gives special attention to "the three," Peter, James, and John, but it appears that he is discipling them all. Mentoring in disciple investing includes bringing another or others along for such activities as visiting those new to the ministry, those in need, or doing outreach or training in small group leadership.

C. Personal Counsel—As mentioned above, counseling has the ability to penetrate the depths of the heart. As a practice, personal counsel, or guidance, can make seismic impressions that can greatly affect an individual's walk through life with Christ. Discussing struggles and helping an individual explore how to approach those issues can be a major facet of one-on-one disciple investing. If the other person listens, is receptive, is held accountable, and responds accordingly (and biblically), behavioral change is possible.

D. Personal Assignment—This area addresses assignments (measurable and accountable responses) given through personal counsel or guidance. If a person is struggling in an area of discipline or disobedience, the disciple investor can recommend some ways to overcome the problems in the coming week(s). Then the two may meet together to follow up and determine whether or not the disciple has accomplished the desired response or task.

E. Mission Trips—These opportunities provide cross-cultural experience and can be life-transforming as the Lord brings humility, servanthood, sacrifice, self-denial, and heart change to the participants' souls. The corporate nature of a mission trip also assures that many persons, as well as many activities, will be shaping disciples into greater Christ-likeness.

F. Service and Mercy—Similar to mission trips and ministry together, acts of service and mercy in the lives of others, particularly those who are needy or disadvantaged, are powerful influences. Engaging in tasks and activities that take disciples out of their comfort zones is a reminder of the work of Jesus as he took on human flesh and ministered to the world through the incarnation.

G. Meals with Others—Food and fellowship together often provide a vibrant avenue for sharing lives, thus enhancing growth in the relationship. A sense of community draws hearts toward one another and opens the door to greater transparency between individuals. The importance of lunches or dinners together for fostering opportunities of Christian growth must not be underestimated. The disciple investor will do well to seek hospitality or fellowship with those who want to grow in Christ and must make every effort not to neglect these crucial ministry meetings.

H. Rebuke and Correction—One of the most difficult ministries in the life of the disciple investor is that of lovingly pointing out the truth about subtle or blatant sins and weaknesses in another follower of Christ. Although sometimes specific groups exist that seem to relish in the ministry of "rebuke" (I once had a neighbor who reportedly constantly rebuked his wife in an authoritarian manner reflecting his religious tradition), ordinarily no one naturally seeks out the avenue of rebuking another. But biblically speaking, there is without question a place for humble, loving rebuke among those in the Christian community. "Pay attention to yourselves! If your brother sins, rebuke him, and if he repents, forgive him" (Luke 17:3). "Do not reprove a scoffer, or he will hate you; reprove a wise man, and he will love you" (Prov 9:8). Rebuke and correction are wonderful "ministers" in the life of the believer. I have been rebuked quite a few times in my life (not including the many appropriate times I have been lovingly rebuked by my wife) and although I never like such encounters, I am deeply grateful for those occasions and for those who would love me enough to help me become more like Jesus!

I. Practicing the Disciplines—There are many habits, practices, or actions that all believers should incorporate into their lives in order to draw closer to or pursue God: fasting, prayer, Bible and other Christian study, worship, journaling, tithing and giving, service, mercy and evangelism, integrating faith into life, Christian reading, etc. These habits are easy for disciples to evaluate. Either they are committed to these practices, struggling with them or forgetting them altogether. And some disciplines can become even more difficult to practice. I was introduced to "half days of prayer" (they actually lasted about three hours, but that was a lot) by the Navigators ministry, and a similar practice ("prayer days," in which the entire campus was shut down) was a part of my seminary life and training at Columbia International University.

As a young Christian and seminary student, I was no stranger to spending extended time in prayer, both corporate and personal. Fasting can be for one meal, one day, or one week (properly prepare yourself for lengthy fasts). Worship and solitude (such as Jesus practiced) can be extended in a personal context if desired. One can set aside extra hours for Bible study or reading Christian books. One can choose to give more than a tithe or dedicate some free time in a sacrificial ministry to others as a means of stewardship. And one can step out of her comfort zone and volunteer for a ministry that is foreign to previous experiences or place and calling in life.

J. Visiting Others—Intentional, personal involvement with and in the lives of others is a potent teacher in learning Christ-like ministry. If the disciple investor takes a disciple or two with him to visit others in their homes, apartments, dorms, offices, or especially the hospital, the interactions and ministry can leave deep impressions on all of the participants. Just hanging out with people also works. The disciple investor will grow, the disciple will grow, and those visited will experience the presence of Christ in their midst.

I found all of the above to be true while an aspiring minister in seminary engaging in two different internships. One pastor who mentored me was the late Dr. Gary Aitken of Covenant Presbyterian Church in Columbia, South Carolina. He made regular, weekly pastoral home visits, usually without scheduling them through appointments. Despite having a congregation of hundreds of people, he often knew what was happening in people's lives; he made it a point to try to visit those who were recovering from hospitalizations, those widowed, or those who had recently gone through some type of trial or crisis.

On the other hand, I was also mentored by the Reverend Dr. Al Lutz, during a summer internship. Pastor Lutz was the consummate pastor. He knew the name of every family member from a church of over 300 people. I once watched him welcome every single person sitting in the Sunday morning worship service by name, pew by pew. He was a shepherd of the flock. He once took me on something that I had never thought of before—business (or office) visits. He knew whom he could find and visit during the work day without disrupting their business too much. He didn't call ahead. He didn't stay very long. But he left an impression on those he visited; they knew he was thinking of them and their Christian responsibilities in the marketplace. And through those visits, he made an obvious impression on me as well. I have often strategically and discerningly stopped by selective people in their place of work, sometimes waiting to see them as if I were another customer. No one ever implied that I ought not to do so after having done so. I was mentored well!

Question of balance: Consider whether your ministry of disciple investing is too behavioral. This consideration causes us to pause as we reflect on this important question: Am I balanced? That is, because you are behaviorally oriented in your personal ministry, do you fail to convey to your disciples the importance of learning and growing in truth and knowledge, and also feeling truth? Or do you simply assume that they are learners and feelers, or worse yet, ignore those two other domains?

8

Balanced Disciple Investing

Preparation for Life

CHARLES JOHNSON READIED HIMSELF in anticipation for the crucial pitches coming in his direction in the top of the tenth inning of the final game of the 1997 World Series, knowing that his team must maintain the 1-1 tie with the Cleveland Indians in order to potentially win the game in their next at bat. Runners were stationed on first and second, but Johnson was prepared. Rob Nen, the star relief pitcher of the Marlins, wound up and delivered a huge breaking curve. However, it dropped about five feet in front of the plate. If the errant pitch got by Johnson, the runners would advance, becoming perilously stationed in scoring position. Johnson handled the wild throw effortlessly. The game, he knew, was safely in his hands. He was ready; he had been there before.

Johnson, one must understand, was the best defensive catcher in the major leagues during the 1997 baseball season, and not by chance. He had been discipled, even groomed, for this situation by his faithful and persistent father. Growing up, Charles' dad would make him put on full catcher's gear, place him in the backyard, and set the pitching machine at a delivery distance of fifty five feet, approximately five feet short of the major league span between the pitcher's mound and home plate. Then Mr. Johnson would constantly send pitch after pitch into the dirt, bouncing and caroming in every direction. Charles had to learn to stop each pitch. As an extra incentive, Charles' dad would promise him a Big Mac if he could stop a hundred pitches in a row. Johnson was motivated, but better yet, through discipline and personal guidance, he was well trained to fulfill the demands of a pressurized major league baseball contest, even the seventh game of the

World Series. He had been discipled well. He was an outstanding product of his father's discipleship program.

Jesus gave his followers one very clear mandate after his resurrection; he could have said many things, but these he had already spoken in his three years spent with them. *One* concern was his focus and he gave *one* command: "Make disciples of all nations . . . teaching them to observe all that I have commanded you" (Matt 28:18–20). Churches have attempted, in many ways, to fulfill Jesus's mandate. Over the years Christians have enacted many models of discipleship and ministry, some executed poorly and others effectively. Scores of Christians have been victorious disciples of Christ while others have floundered. What makes the difference? Who has influenced them? What are the wrong models? Is there a right model?

"Funnel"-mentalism

The purpose and goal of this chapter is to study, describe, and evaluate various models of ministry, using a modified funnel design as a means to understand the implications for creating true and balanced disciples. Through the funnel models, we will attempt to define and describe the problem of creating balanced disciples of Jesus Christ. The various funnel models will also help define imbalanced discipleship processes. We will examine a proper model of ministry as well.

In order to understand whether any model of discipleship is effective, one must first define the goal or end-product desired. What is a disciple? What does a disciple look like? Since we have already considered numerous definitions and requirements for being a disciple earlier, I shall present only a brief definition. Disciples are those who have been born again by the Spirit of God and are new creatures in Christ Jesus. Disciples follow Christ. Discipleship includes learning, heart transformation, and life change. We could list numerous other characteristics of a maturing disciple, but for the sake of brevity, the above definitions will suffice. However, we will describe and expand these three specific, but comprehensive qualities which lead to becoming a balanced disciple—truth, love, and righteousness—later under the description of the "Healthy Model" of discipleship provided below.

I believe discipleship must be balanced in order for disciples to most clearly reflect Jesus and in order for them to grow properly. Firstly, I would submit that believers must be properly taught and believe solid, biblical doctrine; they must know the *truth*. Secondly, believers must recognize that they are loved and accepted by their heavenly Father and respond to that love by loving God with all of their hearts, souls, minds, and strength, and by loving their neighbor as themselves. Healthy disciples must be characterized by *love*. Finally, believers must understand the will of God, expressed by his commands and revealed through biblical principles. As they understand God's will, they must live righteous and faithful lives in all of their relationships, both before God and others; in other words, they must be *righteous* (or Christ-like) in daily living. These three attributes of a disciple will be the focus on the remainder of this chapter and the diagrams contained within it.

Explanation of the Prototype Model (Pictured Below)

Many church models of discipleship exist; some are healthier than others and some inadvertently, but clearly inhibit or restrict the goal of maturity in Christ, which should be the outcome of the discipleship process. The model illustrated in Figure 1 is the prototype for the successive models. This prototype needs a brief word of explanation. The modified funnel design is a picture of the church, God's designated place for discipleship. The church is surrounded by the (unbelieving and pagan) world. The top of the funnel is the *entry point of the church*—it is the church's willingness to proclaim the gospel and receive sinners who have responded through repentance toward God and faith in Jesus Christ (Acts 20:21). It is the point of entry of unbelievers into the visible body of Christ (the local church), where they can meet Christ as Savior and Lord and learn to grow into Christ-likeness. The church must assure a broad entry to the gospel; i.e., it must maintain the forceful message and claims of the gospel, but must not minimize the "whosoever will" invitation and offer by demanding some humanly fabricated stricture. The late Dr. Jack Miller suggests that "the typical static congregation . . . is segregated from the world in all the wrong ways—its members exclude others by the social discipline of a private club."[1] Miller's concern is that the top of the funnel might be narrowed by elitist attitudes. Such concern is not unwarranted, as we shall see later, since elitism and other attitudes can cause the top of the funnel to become too narrow. Surprisingly, it can also become too wide.

The sides of the funnel are curved to symbolize that there is a *molding process* occurring; the new believer should not be independent of or

1. Miller, *Outgrowing the Ingrown Church*, 46.

unattached to the body of Christ but is shaped and formed by the life, ministry, people, and methods of the local church. Dr. Donald MacNair states that the two primary tasks of the church are evangelism—in order that the lost may be found through the gospel of Christ, and growth in grace—that the members of Christ's body may grow up to be like him through the means of grace he has given them.[2] This molding process (with its goal of growth in grace) involves teaching and instruction, oversight and accountability, interdependent relationships, training, and many additional avenues to provide help and guidance toward such growth. The top and the sides of the funnel symbolize these two primary tasks.

Furthermore, the curvature of the sides signifies the active movement of new believers into the life-giving body of believers. They must receive follow-up and be incorporated (or assimilated) into the body in order to prevent spiritual atrophy. Robert Coleman, in his classic book, *The Master Plan of Evangelism*, submits that where there exists haphazard follow-up of believers, it is no wonder that about half of those who make professions and join the church eventually fall away (note: he is an Arminian), or lose the glow of a Christian experience; fewer still grow in sufficient knowledge and grace to be of any real service to the Kingdom.[3] Finally, the sides indicate the style of the molding process. Will it be rigid or flexible, strict or loose, heavy-handed or helpful?

Again, what is the goal of the molding process? The discipling church will produce healthy Christians and they will therefore glorify God, according to Bill Hull.[4] Any deviation in the sides will create an unhealthy and *imbalanced* believer. Paul mentions some rigid control systems of belief and behavior in the book of Colossians. These systems of belief warp the congregation (the funnel/discipleship mold), thus adversely affecting the disciple (his maturity and re-entry). Briefly, these control systems are: legalism, which places law over love (Col 2:16); mysticism, which replaces the need for revealed truth (Col 2:18); and asceticism, which is a false form of righteousness (Col 2:20–23). The relevance of these false systems will gain more value when the healthy model is observed. Any imbalance in the funnel will hinder the disciple in maturity and will create a dysfunctional follower who will inevitably lack some aspect of Christ-likeness.

---

2. MacNair, *The Living Church*, 21.
3. Coleman, *The Master Plan of Evangelism*, 49.
4. Hull, *The Complete Book of Discipleship*, 157.

This imbalance and its attendant shortcomings will create obvious problems at the bottom end of the funnel, which symbolizes the *relationship of growing and maturing believers with their world* (i.e., their re-entry, so to speak, into their world). By the phrase *the world* we are speaking of the unbelieving world in which the disciple presently lives. Of course, in the discipleship process, disciples are always relating to their former lives and world (sometimes precariously), but the bottom of the funnel depicts the goal (which, admittedly, is not fully attainable, but a goal nonetheless) of producing a mature follower of Christ who can relate to and function in (and hopefully lead in) the often hostile and resistant world in which they live. Hull summarizes the importance of this "re-entry" into the world from the perspective of kingdom thinking when he says, "The kingdom thinker (disciple making pastor) says, 'We are taking the rule of Christ to the world. What you are in the world for Christ is most important.'"[5] Mike Regele, in his poignant text, *Death of the Church*, underscores Hull's opinion when he suggests, ". . . the individual members of the local congregation are the primary agents of mission. We have the opportunity to again reimagine the lay person as playing not just a supporting actor role but a lead role in the mission of Christ's church in the world."[6] The mature disciple should be a Christ-like follower who leads in the world; a missionary of sorts. This mission role is the hope of re-entry. C. Peter Wagner summarizes the funnel design by stating three priorities of healthy growing churches (parentheses mine, providing explanation):

- Priority One: Commitment to Christ (Top: Point of entry, out of the world and into the church, [through conversion])
- Priority Two: Commitment to the Body of Christ (Sides: The discipleship process)
- Priority Three: Commitment to the work of Christ in the world (Bottom: Re-entry into the world)[7]

---

5. Hull, *The Disciple Making Church*, 108.
6. Regele, *Death of the Church*, 220.
7. Wagner, *Your Church Can Grow*, 187.

FIGURE ONE
THE PROTOTYPE MODEL

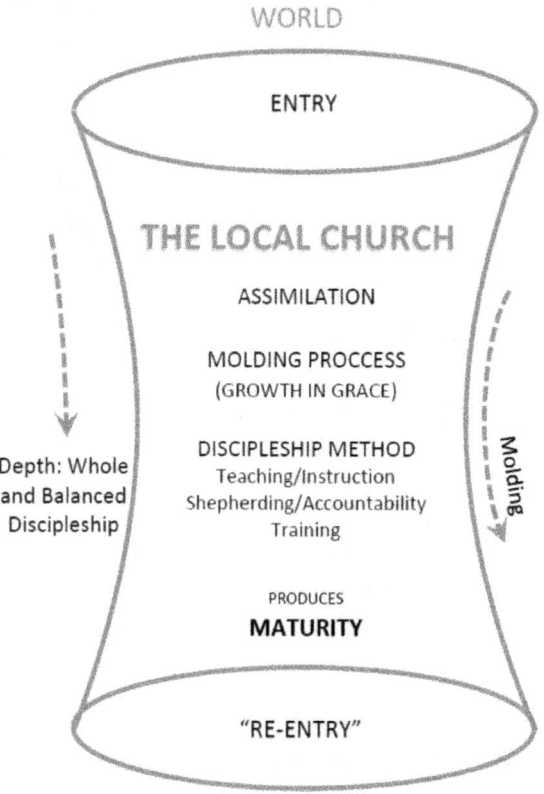

Imbalanced Models

The Imbalanced Truth Model

The Truth Model is imbalanced because of its narrowness and rigidity, particularly in its doctrinal perspective and instruction (see Figure 2). The entry or entrance to the church or ministry is both narrow because the gospel is defined in a narrow fashion and because of the apparent narrowness that outsiders perceive as they view the members of the congregation. The gospel, as defined by the Truth Model, might indeed be "repent and believe," as it should be, but one must also accept or believe the Truth Church's strong and often distinctive convictions as well. Furthermore, some truth models require those who join them to have full understanding of its doctrinal distinctions before one can really believe and become a member. The gospel, as truth and doctrine, is given such preeminence and importance that it takes precedence over the loving relationships that can enhance the church's winsomeness. Thus, this environment of truth without love creates an uninviting imbalance. Outsiders perceive the Truth Church as unconcerned for others and smug. It resembles an esoteric club with rigid entrance requirements, summarized in a code of beliefs. Since truth is all that (apparently) matters, the entry (funnel top) appears narrow. There is no room for disagreement in the areas of Scripture that are not clear, i.e., the gray areas. Theological narrowness characterizes this church. Love is often lacking.

Michael Griffiths quotes Francis Schaeffer in this regard, "We must ask, *Do I fight merely for doctrinal faithfulness?* This is like the wife who never sleeps with anybody else, but never shows love to her own husband. Is that a sufficient relationship in marriage? No, ten thousand times, no!"[8] This unloving church will be rigid in its discipleship of its members, if it can indoctrinate them easily. Only one perspective, i.e., the truth to which it adheres dearly, is taught and typifies its disciples. Suspicion reigns in this church. The members, in particular, question the doctrinal integrity and credibility of outsiders who do not hold to *their* grasp of the truth of the Scriptures. However, the Truth Church's greatest danger may be within, as members easily become suspicious of one another, thus potentially fragmenting the church. Churches, as is well documented, most usually split because of poor relationships, not doctrinal differences.

Such are the disciples in this model; they are relationally unhealthy and thus imbalanced. Their re-entry into the world is narrow as well; their relations with others are stiff and rigid because of a mind-set of suspicion and an inability to be flexible and loving toward others. If the Truth Church is saturated with lots of teaching and doctrine and becomes a teaching only church, the results are disastrous. Disciples become pregnant with knowledge and lessen their effectiveness with unbelievers. Their knowledge, without the balance of practice, becomes an encumbrance and they lose sight of the real needs of people in the world around them (see inset

---

8. Griffiths, *God's Forgetful Pilgrims*, 80.

in Figure 2). Examples of the Truth Church abound. We commonly know these groups as fighting (or militant) fundamentalists, "T.R." (thoroughly Reformed) Presbyterians, doctrinal separatists, the extreme right, and we should also include the historic, so-called nondenominational Church of Christ. I'm sure there must be others representing every denominational tradition and heritage.

FIGURE TWO
IMBALANCED MODELS

Model 1:
The TRUTH MODEL – "NARROW/NARROW"

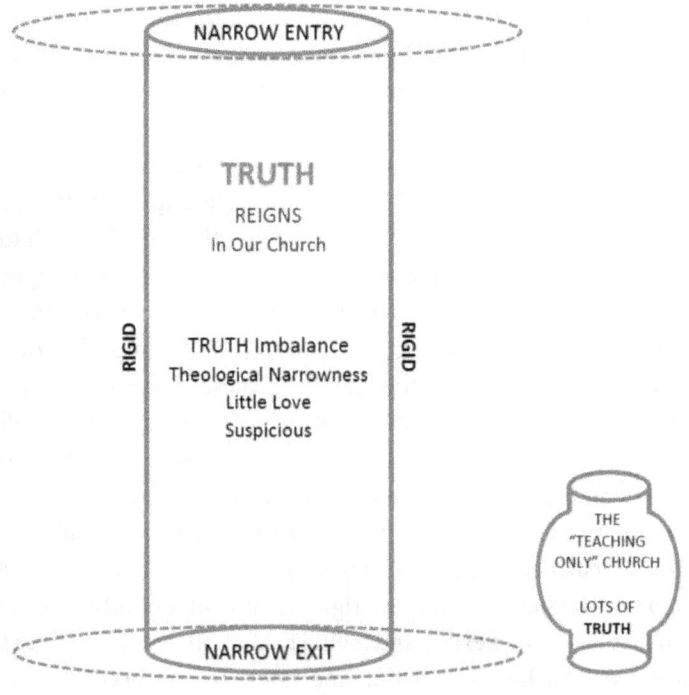

The Imbalanced Righteousness Model

The Righteousness Model (see Figure 3) is quite similar to the Truth Model in that it too has an unnecessarily narrow entry and contains a rigid style of discipleship. I believe, however, that the Righteousness Model is more dangerous and destructive than the Truth Model because of the great self-deception that attends self-righteousness. This model potentially closes off relationships with the world in the re-entry end of the funnel and encourages an unhealthy disdain for the world (hating and despising), one that renders the believer almost completely ineffective with outsiders. The need to sustain one's own righteousness impels believers to avoid any "filth" unbelievers might inadvertently transfer to them, and to beware of potential scandal awaiting them "out there in the world." Therefore, as they will not or cannot easily relate to the unbelieving world, the bottom of the funnel is nearly closed.

This discipleship model includes both adherence to rigid truth statements and strict standards of righteous living. Discipleship is defined by purity, as well as by looking better than you once were, or better than the next person. This imbalanced model may profess justification by faith and Christ's imputed righteousness as a means of acceptance before God, but the reality is that followers do not trust Christ completely (and possibly not at all) for their salvation. It is a sad state of affairs and makes for a poor disciple. I know; I've not only seen it—I've lived it!

There exists in the lives of these disciples a lack of true love; they have not been set free by the love and work of Christ. They are dependent upon *the system* of the church, whether it be the moral standards of the church or some other superimposed authority. In this regard, Allen Hadidian, author of *Successful Discipling,* submits, "This is the sobering aspect of example: your disciples will reproduce not only your strengths, but also your weaknesses."[9] The system of the righteousness model is fraught with weakness and produces weak and ineffective disciples. False righteousness begets itself and insecurity abounds, while being clothed in a projection of outward self-confidence and security. Rigid shepherding (oversight control by leaders) is frequently introduced so as to reassure disciples that they are *doing* the right thing. Often this authoritative example is the only model from which poor, fledgling disciples may learn or follow. Reproduction and multiplication, sadly, continue an ugly cycle. Examples of this

---

9. Hadidian, *Successful Discipling,* 54.

model might be strict fundamentalism, old-time Pentecostalism, charismatic extremism, various extremist sects and cults, and unfortunately at times, even the evangelical victorious Christian life, deeper life, and higher life camps with their expectations of near perfection of the will and outward conformity and behavior.

FIGURE THREE
IMBALANCED MODELS

Model 2:
The RIGHTEOUSNESS MODEL – "NARROW/CLOSED"

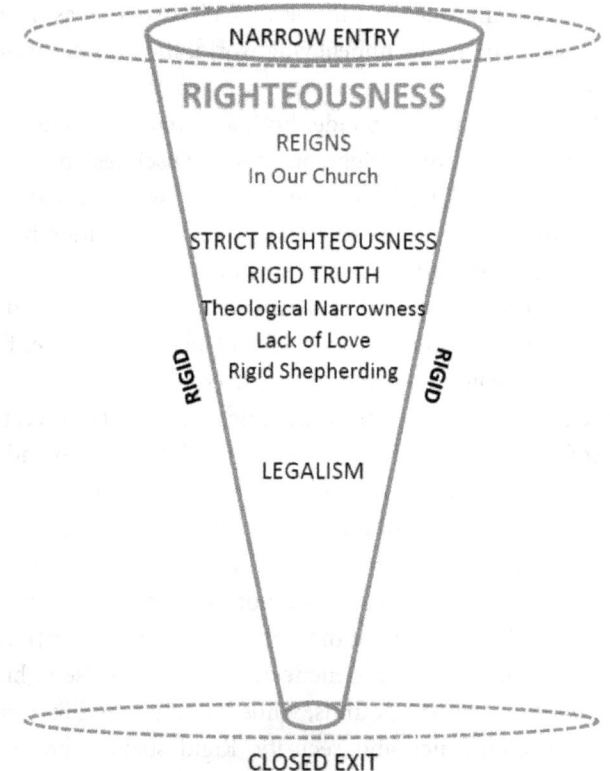

The Imbalanced Love Model

This model (see Figure 4), although potentially the weakest as a disciple producing model, is probably the most popular model existing today in American culture. The reason for its popularity is based upon its weakness—it builds a large and impressive church in regard to externals, particularly concerning numbers and prominence. This church emphasizes the goal of being the most loving church possible and is therefore perceived as the most open and accepting. Therefore, people are drawn to its openness and tolerance. The entry point (top of the funnel) is broader (or wider) than any other, yet its breadth is its weakness. It is sensitive to seekers, those who have previously been turned off to or turned out of the church, or those who have never been very involved in a church at all. It opens the door widely for them to come and explore the faith. That is the strength (and weakness) of the Love Model. Often, people come in droves. Attendance is impressive. These inquirers (or seekers) have little to lose by coming because the demands are not great. They are not confronted directly with the claims of Christ, although, in all sincerity, the church usually wishes to help these seekers find Christ at some point in the process.

Love and acceptance is the motto of this congregation. Tolerance may be another shingle that they hang out for all to see. What can be *experienced* is often the attraction that draws inquirers. In order to secure a greater audience, this model minimizes truth (the claims of Christ to us) and righteousness (the claims of Christ upon us). It requires strong, wise, and skillful leadership in order to produce more than a small circle of real disciples in this context. Usually it does not meet these requirements and it does not happen. Evangelism is frequently the goal of this model and an inherent and reluctant acceptance of weak discipleship is often the result. Dietrich Bonhoeffer saw this model in his day, and addressed it in his classic work, *The Cost of Discipleship* when he spoke of "cheap grace" (i.e., following Christ costs nothing). Some years ago, I encountered a potential staff member of such a church who was considering working in the area of women's discipleship. She remarked that her pastor reflected on the state of their church by saying, "We are a mile wide (*broad entry*) and an inch deep (*short funnel*)." At least he recognized the problem! Worship (sometimes very slick worship), music, and preaching are often very well executed; first impressions are vital and the model emphasizes great presentation (in a front-door outreach method). The funnel is shallow because the discipleship and the disciples are shallow. Often only persistent seekers receive training and undergo the maturing process.

At the bottom of the funnel, the re-entry is small because the model only produces a minimal number of true, mature disciples who have been enabled to touch their world. Yet this world is the real world, which needs the touch of Christ-like followers. Churches that reflect this model might possibly be large, fast-growing Baptist and charismatic churches, or the plethora of "seeker church" or "seeker friendly" congregations that began in the late 1980s. Some large churches around the world, however, actually work to prevent the Love Model and its shallow funnel by providing a vast and organized system of small group discipleship for the bulk of their members. They are to be commended for their efforts.

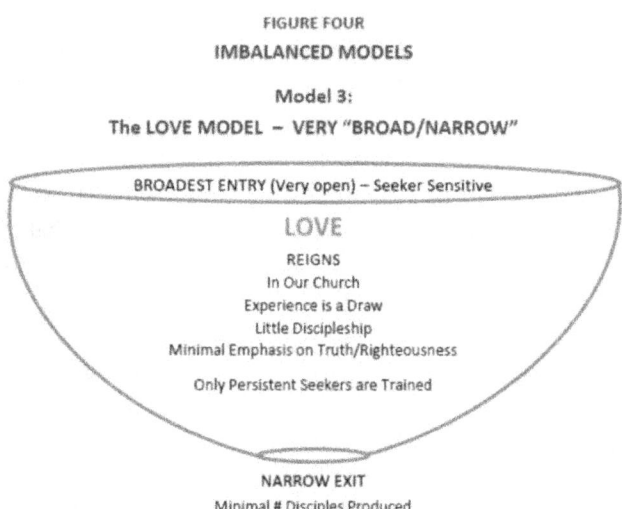

FIGURE FOUR
IMBALANCED MODELS
Model 3:
The LOVE MODEL – VERY "BROAD/NARROW"

BROADEST ENTRY (Very open) – Seeker Sensitive
LOVE
REIGNS
In Our Church
Experience is a Draw
Little Discipleship
Minimal Emphasis on Truth/Righteousness
Only Persistent Seekers are Trained

NARROW EXIT
Minimal # Disciples Produced

The Imbalanced High Demand Model

The High Demand Model (see Figure 5) is a simple one to explain. It can be found in many places but is actually predominant outside of the local church. Parachurch ministries are able to use it successfully because they are independent (little accountability besides themselves), highly selective, don't need to deal with every type of person and age category (highly specialized), and are able to set their own standards, which are frequently quite high in order to fulfill their specific mission and reach their particular goals. Only the truly committed and serious need apply! As mentioned above (Chapter Seven: military discipleship), these are the *marines* of the kingdom, exploring and conquering the fortresses of Satan. The High Demand Model usually has a broad entry point and is open to anyone; it might even specialize in evangelism and outreach. But often the goal is to surface movers, shakers, and potential leaders, so the sides of the funnel become narrow quickly. This narrowing effect may produce some highly motivated, well-trained, mature, and effective disciples, but in the process a tragic side effect occurs: the weaker and more frail members are challenged beyond their abilities or are simply left behind. The High Demand Model actually creates a culture that is exclusive and potentially elitist, a very unbiblical position to hold.

In essence, this model squeezes these "lesser" believers out of the discipleship process (hopefully inadvertently) and frequently out of the group (or church). The standards and demands intimidate and overwhelm the "average" believer, leaving him with a sense of second-class citizenship in the kingdom. This rigid discipleship approach might include demands such as fasting, extensive Scripture memory, giving well above the tithe, required shepherding and submission, reading the Bible through in a year, weekly stranger ("cold-turkey") evangelism, attendance at all church meetings, and numerous other requirements. Many of the above activities are good and helpful in themselves and enhance the maturation of the believer, but they can become dangerous when they are an end in themselves or they become the measurement of Christian faith to the extreme, as well as the expected and normal standard of one's daily Christian life.

FIGURE FIVE
IMBALANCED MODELS

Model 4:
The HIGH DEMAND MODEL – "BROAD/NARROW"

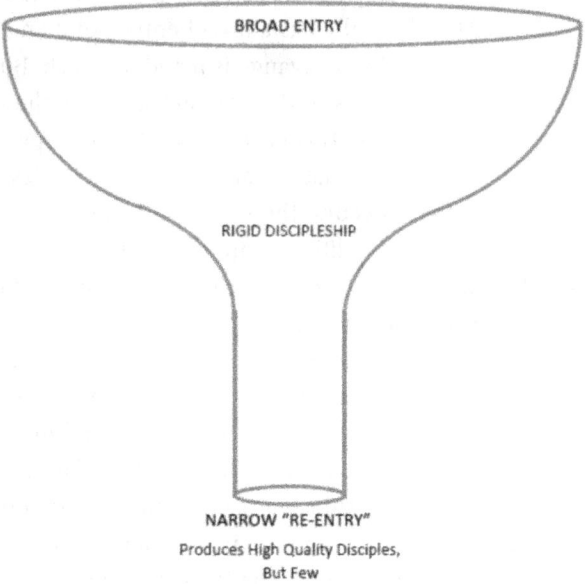

Produces High Quality Disciples,
But Few

The Impossible Model

This model (see Figure 6) simply will not work. It begins with a narrow entry which restricts membership initially; it is exclusionary. Limited outreach hinders growth and vision so that no matter what type of discipleship process (sides) is included, the exit (bottom) cannot be wide. It produces few real disciples, if any. The Impossible Model can become the Narrow/Narrow Model (the Truth Model) or the Narrow/Closed Model (the Righteousness Model), but the narrow entry will not produce an open or broad re-entry. The fact that a narrow entry point is unhealthy and leads to a cult-like environment consisting of false truth, rigid righteousness (and regimentation), and phony love makes it impossible to produce Christ-like followers in any fashion or any strength.

FIGURE SIX
IMBALANCED MODELS

Model 5:
The IMPOSSIBLE MODEL – "NARROW/BROAD"

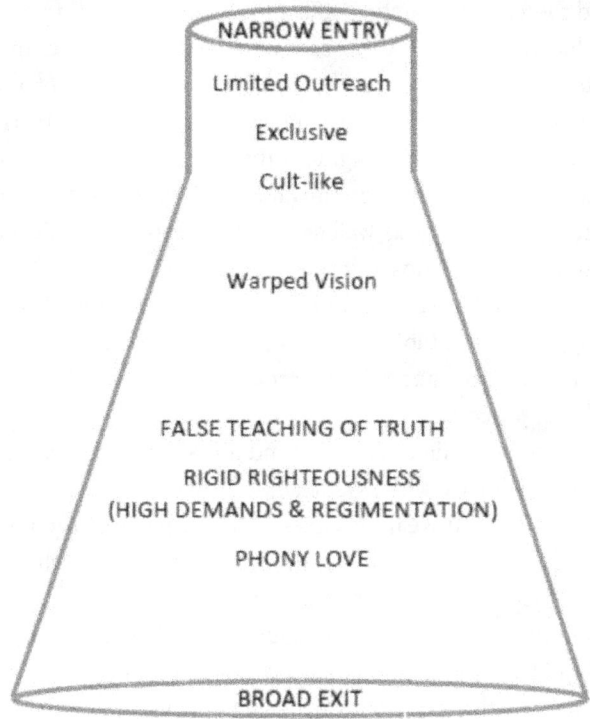

The Balanced Model

This Balanced Model is proposed as the ideal model of discipleship, since, in reality, no perfect model can possibly exist. The ideal is presented as a healthy model because it ought to produce mature, reproducing disciples of Jesus Christ who can contribute to the life and ministry of the local church and also relate to, function in, contribute to, and influence their world, i.e., the unbelieving world around them. The entry is broad; the gospel is to be presented to all the world. Believers are assimilated upon repentance and profession of faith in the finished work of Christ on the cross. Covenant children (children of believing parents) are assimilated by virtue of the faith of their parents (or parent), although as potential covenant breakers they can exit out of the body (funnel). Whole person discipleship (mind, will, and emotion) is the goal of the molding process and the whole person must therefore be discipled in a balanced fashion. Henrichsen suggests, regarding the building process, ". . . here we seek to change the man's sense of values, and thereby ultimately to affect his whole personality."[10]

This balanced molding process occurs through an emphasis upon what the apostle John, in his first letter, states are the marks of a true believer: truth (2:20–23); love (2:10–11); and righteousness (2:3–6). Truth comes through the teaching, preaching, and instruction of the word and sound doctrine, as well as through worship and the sacraments. Love comes from the corporate community, as well as through relationships developed with individuals, in small groups and elsewhere as relationships flourish. Righteousness is a natural bi-product of truth and love through the working of the Holy Spirit. Accountability (one-on-one and small group accountability), personal attention, and support produce maturity, holiness, and purity in the molding process.

As mentioned earlier, unhealthy and unbalanced models often replace love with legalism, truth with mysticism, and righteousness with asceticism; they produce false and weak disciples. Other aspects of the molding process include ministry skill training and gift discovery, as well as increasing knowledge of God, self, and others. Maturity (i.e., growing in Christ-like character) in the whole person is produced as the lives of Christ-following believers (and learners) find transformation in mind (gaining the mind of Christ through truth), emotions (growing in the love of Christ for God and others), and will (learning the conduct of Christ as they grow in righteousness and holiness). The sides of the funnel appear to be narrowing but this narrowing effect is only a symbol or picture of the *molding* which is bringing about change among the disciples.

This change is actually *broadening* disciples through a process of balanced sanctification and is thus preparing them for re-entry into life in the world (so to speak—they are always relating to the world in which God has placed them). Ideally, this balanced funnel model is constantly preparing those in the discipleship process to be able to minister within the local church body and to relate to the lost world in which they live. As Ray Stedman submits in his revolutionary text (of that day), *Body Life*, "The church,

---

10. Henrichsen, *Disciples Are Made*, 73.

therefore, when it lives in and by the Spirit, is to be nothing more or less than the extension of the life of Jesus to the whole world in any age."[11] The process of discipleship, of course, is never complete. Similarly, the process of sanctification is never completed here on earth, but both disciple investing and sanctification imply both growth and change. The bottom line is that maturity and Christ-likeness can occur through the healthy model. And, by God's grace, it capably prepares mature disciples to serve both in Jesus's church and to extend the life of Jesus to the whole world. Through the discipline and personal guidance of their father's faithful presence, disciples, like Charles Johnson, seasoned major league catcher, are well-trained to live for Christ in a pressurized world.

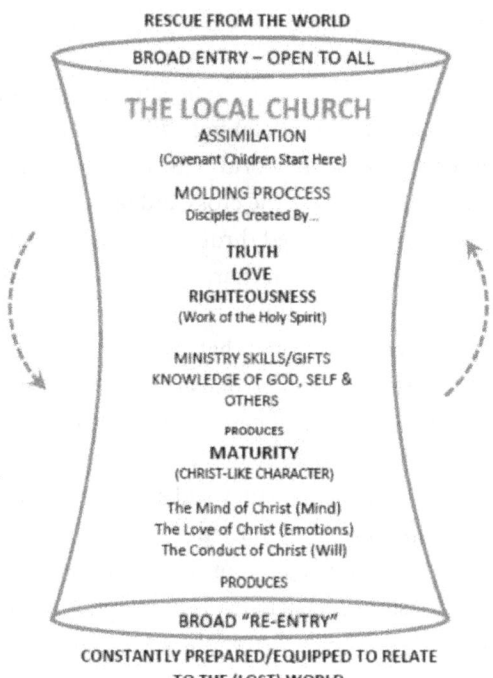

FIGURE SEVEN
THE BALANCED MODEL

Model 6:
The HEALTHY MODEL – "BROAD/BROAD"

11. Stedman, *Body Life: The Church Comes Alive*, 38.

9

Working it out in Ministry

Review

IN ITS ESSENCE, DISCIPLE investing is biblical, time and labor intensive, and strategic. It is biblical because, in his Great Commission, Christ commanded his original disciples (and I believe, his followers throughout the ages) to make disciples of all nations. It is time and labor intensive because growth in Christ-likeness and holiness does not occur overnight, nor does it happen without struggle, wrestling, self-denial, commitment, and perseverance. It is strategic because making disciples is the method Christ prescribed in order to reach the world with the good news of grace and forgiveness found in his death on the cross and in his resurrection.

Thus far, we have both worked through various definitions of disciple making, noted some Old Testament characteristics of followers of God, and learned about the ministry of disciple investing from Paul's heart cries to the church at Galatia. We have noted that certain influences undergird the disciple influencing process, such as one's church tradition or denomination (if applicable), one's own local church or ministry, and one's own personal preferences. Then we noted that when people seek to build disciple investing relationships with others, they will encounter a variety of possible receptions. The disciple investor must discern the level of resistance or interest and the individual's needs in order to proceed properly. Building a meaningful relationship is crucial to the process.[1] We also considered numerous philosophical approaches to the disciple investing process and

---

1. The primary means for discerning where people are in their spiritual interest and progress is derived as the disciple investor engages in the art of diagnosis, i.e., asking questions to determine the spiritual needs in a person's soul. Once the area of need is determined, the most logical starting point is to provide scriptural help and instruction.

addressed the need for preventing both imbalanced disciple investing and imbalanced disciples.

Proposal

What I propose to do in this chapter is to suggest some strategies for working out the disciple investing process in actual ministry. I will consider both campus ministry and the church pastorate, as well as what to do if you are a committed layperson wishing to pursue this path of discipleship. I will *not* provide a framework or program for building or creating disciples of Christ. As I attempt to build a philosophy of ministry that supports disciple investing, I certainly encourage readers to determine if this ministry philosophy is suitable to their own present or future ministries. I will also try to provide some brief descriptions of the practice of disciple investing on the campus and in the local church, some of which I have only seen from a distance rather than firsthand.

The Power of a Book

I fully admit that my approach to both kingdom building and disciple investing was heavily influenced while in college at the University of South Carolina. And although I was impacted by the campus ministry of the Navigators, and by my lengthy tenure in Campus Crusade for Christ (Cru), the primary life-changing influence that changed my perspective about discipleship came from reading a book. In spite of all of the investing that others had done for me, including an immersion into a heavy military discipleship method (Navigators) and a truly programmatic and systematic discipleship method (Cru), the greatest enlightenment that I received was from an intense reading of a relatively short book. That book was written by then Asbury Seminary professor, Dr. Robert E. Coleman, and entitled *The Master Plan of Evangelism*.

Without trying to explain the contents of this landmark book, I can summarize it by expressing that it has had a greater impact upon both my ministry and my ministry philosophy than any other book I have ever read outside of the Bible. I have read it numerous times and taught through it often. Dr. Coleman insightfully addresses the method that Jesus used in order to reach the world with the gospel. Divided into eight succinct chapters and based primarily on the New Testament gospel accounts, the basic premise of the book is that disciples of Christ are made by taking significant time to invest in them personally, rather than simply focusing upon the numbers and the masses (contrary to how we usually think in our western culture). Coleman also makes a pivotal suggestion, one that requires a faith leap on the part of anyone involved in the disciple investing process: *the discipler must recognize that the efforts put into investing in others may not bear fruit until years later.* It is not the present results that count but the future product and fruitfulness (often unseen by the discipler) that a disciple investor must consider when placing time, energy, and relational effort into building both disciples and leaders in the kingdom. Jesus had only one plan to reach the world with the news of the kingdom of heaven, and that plan was to entrust its success into the hands of a small group of inadequate and insufficient men. Such an approach is profound, as seemingly it will not work. Ultimately however, Jesus selected, associated with, led, taught, mentored, and delegated his work and vision to a handful of men (men who might be termed "suspect") and then left them behind to reproduce all that he had taught them and given them. The rest is history.

One Person Can Change the World

The Master Plan of Evangelism will challenge the local church pastor, the person in ministry or on the mission field, and the person in the pew to think through the question, "In whom am I directly investing so that they might know Christ better?" Don't be deceived by numbers. Rather, assess ministry success by judging the reality of Christ-likeness in the lives of those who name the name of Christ. That premise is the beauty of *The Master Plan of Evangelism*. Upon reading *The Master Plan of Evangelism* the first time, I realized that ministry numbers were not always an indicator of personal spiritual realities. Of course, I had seen this in my own experience in attending a large Southern Baptist Church. Not everyone who was attending was there to worship God (the "balconeers" for instance, those sitting in the balcony strategically present in a pre-eHarmony method of mate selection). I had watched our Cru ministry at the University of South Carolina increase its staff and demand more commitment, yet student involvement had shrunk. I often wondered if my ascent to student leadership was one of the reasons for our loss of growth. Numbers were down and I wondered if God was still working.

WORKING IT OUT IN MINISTRY

As a college student involved in a struggling campus ministry, I had to ponder and pray deeply while asking the question, "What really matters in ministry?" *The Master Plan* helped me answer that question simply by looking at what really mattered to Jesus and what ultimately matters to God, i.e., individual heart transformation. Such heart transformation derives from honestly dealing with the Scriptures in a context of pouring oneself into others. This is how one person can help change the world and build Christ's kingdom on earth. What was it that I bought into from *The Master Plan*? I will never forget this convincing statement:

> Here is where we must begin just like Jesus. It will be slow, tedious, painful and probably unnoticed by men at first, but the end result will be glorious, even if we don't live to see it. Seen in this way, though, it becomes a big decision in ministry. One must decide where he wants his ministry to count – in the momentary applause of popular recognition or in the reproduction of his life in a few chosen men who will carry on his work after he has gone. Really, it is a question of which generation we are living for?[2]

As a senior college student, I bought into Dr. Coleman's conclusions, that Jesus builds his kingdom through personal and intensive investment in a few. I realized that whatever I do in ministry (and I was not yet called to full-time, lifetime ministry at the time), even if it is small, is important to God. That was a revolutionary thought. Additionally, any effort I might give to other individuals to help move them closer to the Lord and toward Christ-likeness is consequential. I did not conclude that numbers are meaningless (the book of Acts is a testament to the undeniable, significant growth of the early church) but statistics need to be kept in their place and in perspective. I believe Coleman was correct when he said, "One must decide where he wants his ministry to count . . ."

I have written all of the above to explain the background of what I am about to propose as far as how to implement a strategy for disciple investing in any ministry. If the reader agrees with Jesus's method (or his "master plan") of evangelism, as well as the concept of focusing upon a few as the strategy for building Christ's kingdom, then I believe that my thoughts in this chapter will make sense. If, however, the reader is not convinced of Coleman's premise, then my thoughts might not be as relevant. I hope they will be helpful nonetheless.

2. Ibid., 37.

As mentioned in Chapter 7, there are three avenues of ministry available for implementing the ministry of disciple investing. I might begin by suggesting that every person who reads this book will gravitate toward one avenue more than the other two. For those who lean toward one-on-one ministry, my proposal will resonate. For those who love preaching, teaching, and speaking to large groups, the other two avenues will appear to be challenges. For some, public speaking appears too challenging or fearful, and one-on-one ministry might be relationally intimidating. (As an aside and possible encouragement: when surveyed, speaking in public is the number one fear for people, just ahead of handling snakes.) Those in this category are the people who avoid large group ministry, yet love and gravitate toward the interaction, discussion, banter, and personal touch of small groups. Individuals must be honest with their own abilities, skills, personalities, and preferences. By observing both Jesus's and the Apostle Paul's ministries, we glean from their practices that while they both spoke publicly to large groups, both spent considerable time with multiple individuals. And of course, Jesus spent the bulk of his ministry with a small group of disciples which at times became smaller (Peter, James, and John).

In Campus Ministry

So, how does someone in ministry implement an emphasis on disciple investing as a way of life for the group?[3] In my experience with campus ministry, I discovered that although my semesters were times of intensive ministry (a compact 15–16 weeks consisting of countless opportunities for varied ministry), as a campus minister I was personally able to carry out the work in which I was engaged in all three avenues of ministry. I taught in a weekly large group setting on campus, which I loved, though it brought much more pressure due to handling the dynamics of a large group. (Our large group was not actually that large but the dynamic was certainly that of a large group.) In addition to large group preaching and teaching, I usually led at least three small groups (sometimes four, with two on Monday nights) during the week. I tried to schedule 10–15, one-on-one appointments per week with students in all of the categories mentioned above in chapter 5: I met with non-Christians (when possible), student contacts (strangers)

---

3. I should also point out that Dr. Bill Hull has written two excellent works that address this question at far greater length than I will, *The Disciple Making Pastor* and *The Disciple Making Church*.

that were referred to me, new students on campus, students visiting our large group (or small group) as a means of follow up, student leaders, rising/potential student leaders, students needing counseling, and sometimes students dealing with conflict. I have to add that I pretty much loved all of those meetings except for the "no shows" who agreed to meet but stood me up (and there were quite a few of those in the student referral category).

A Way of Life

All this to say that even in the midst of the busy semesters of campus ministry, disciple investing was a way of life for me. I was investing in numerous students in all three avenues of ministry, investing in different ways, to differing degrees (of understanding), and on different topics. In many ways, I think this situation is every minister's dream, i.e., spending the bulk of your time applying the truths of Scripture pastorally to people who want to listen and learn. The college student dynamic is unique. Students might be growing in independence and learning self-sufficiency, and though they may be attitudinally resistant and potentially suspicious of others, they are usually teachable and receptive. There are lots of teachable moments on campus. These occur in one-on-one settings, during small groups, and particularly after large group meetings (in either unplanned one-on-one or small group contexts). The most liberating facet of campus ministry is the "freedom" that students' schedules allow. So, on the college campus, I believe that a deliberative approach or effort toward disciple investing on the part of a campus minister or campus staff person is relatively easy. It is why you exist and it is how you function.

Most campus ministries give priority to personal student contact. As a matter of fact, I believe, that for many campus ministries, the large group meeting, whether it is a worship service, a teaching time, a fellowship group, or a service project (or a combination of these possibilities) is often designed to draw students for the more important purposes of meeting and following up with them individually. Most student ministries, unless their purpose is purely "presentational" in scope (as the Fellowship of Christian Athletes [FCA]), have hopes that their large group activities will serve as a place to trigger the formation of either small group meetings or personal, individual follow up with students. This philosophical campus ministry cornerstone, in some ways, is what sets most campus or college ministry efforts apart from what happens in the local church. The specialization of campus ministries, whether parachurch or not, normally enables the staff and ministers to focus upon a Bible-centered teaching ministry characterized by lots of individual contact with students. This scenario is far different in the local church, where at the least it takes a lot more work and effort to make it happen.

Transition from Campus to Church

Tensions

When I changed ministries and moved from the campus (after almost ten years there) to the local church (for church planting), I discovered that my schedule was far more challenging if I wanted to carry forth a ministry focusing upon individual encounters. On a personal basis, having four children under age seven made managing a schedule more difficult than previously. Also, being the senior pastor, I sensed a greater desire from the young families in our church to have family activities together (they actually wanted to do this with their pastor), sometimes during the week. Thus, I was definitely drawn into making family outings, as well as my own children's sports and activities a higher priority for my personal presence. Ultimately, there is a principle involved in marriage and family life that supersedes ministry priorities: the pastor must schedule one-on-one time with his wife and children as much as possible. Similarly, the pastor must view family gatherings as committed "small group" time with those who are dear to him/her. I'm not sure if I succeeded or failed in those priorities and efforts but I do know that I did not ignore my family while under the throes of church planting.

Prior to beginning our church plant, I committed myself before the Lord that should my church plant fall apart (it didn't), I would not let my family fall apart. I am explaining this family/church tension in order to submit that a growing family made my one-on-one contact with individuals in my church (as opposed to student meetings on campus) more difficult to schedule. Scheduling individual meetings with men in the church also drew competition from the hospitality-type dinners that my wife, Cathy, and I would often host in our home. We had a priority of working with couples when possible, as we believed this would be invaluable in building a ministry to the younger couples we were trying to reach. Lastly, and possibly the most obvious deterrent to meeting with men in the local church, is the hurdle of scheduling. Unlike college students, who are available from 7:00 am (not their preference) until potentially midnight (not normal but possible), men in the church, at best, have three or four times during the week to meet individually with someone who is interested in investing in their spiritual growth.

Individual Meetings

In the church, I discovered that I could meet with most men either for breakfast most weekday mornings, lunch most weekdays, maybe late afternoons (depending upon their job), and Saturday mornings if my children didn't have their numerous sports or other activities at that time. Those options were truly limiting compared to being able to meet with college students any time that they weren't in class (or in bed). As I therefore address this issue of disciple investing in the local church, I will admit that for me personally it became a bigger challenge. Additionally, as a church planter, though I did meet with men in the church, I was in essence, in charge of preaching, recruiting, and training officers. I was also involved in hospital (and some home) visitation, was the administrator for an office with one part-time secretary (I had at least three of those in the first four years), and eventually a pastoral assistant. I also served as the visionary and overseer of all of the outreach/evangelism efforts, a regular Sunday School teacher, and a liaison to the administrators of the middle school in which the church met. I'm sure there were other duties as well. In reality, I did almost all of the same things when I served as a campus minister but in those blissful days I had breaks—summer breaks (to some extent—the ministry continued vibrantly as a student-led work), and a break between the fall and spring semesters. The change of pace in an academic calendar was very refreshing, even when there were personal and family trips required for training, support raising, denominational meetings, and vacations (almost always involving trips with the entire family). As a local church pastor, I felt much more restrained from holding one-on-one meetings with men because it seemed the pressures were greater and the duties were larger.

Transfer of Philosophy

This brings me to the place for some discussion about how I "transferred" my RUF campus ministry philosophy into my life and ministry as a pastor in the local church. Firstly, I want to revisit *The Master Plan of Evangelism*. If I believed that investing in a smaller group of people was (at least potentially) more strategic than investing in a large group of people, how would this work out in the local church? I had to grapple with the reality that now that I was in the local church, my meeting times with men were more limited than they had been with male students. I was also forced to think through my RUF training, particularly regarding how the campus minister spends his time meeting with individual students. With whom do you meet? Who is your priority? How do you spend your time and upon what do you focus? And then there was the question regarding developmental stages in life. The male college student is different from the adult male, particularly if the adult male is married, has children, and is working a full-time job.[4] All of those factors in the adult male's life entail added responsibility, pressure, stress, and possible distraction from spiritual realities. With all of these factors in mind, and never having done this type of disciple investing in the local church setting (particularly with men who would be my peers or older), I knew that working out a philosophy of disciple investing would be a challenge.

Selection

Nevertheless, the principles I had learned from *The Master Plan of Evangelism*, as well as those I had gleaned from my training and service with Reformed University Fellowship, were extremely beneficial. From Dr. Coleman's book, I had indeed become convinced that the first step in discipling other men, as Jesus demonstrated, was "selection." Jesus chose certain men to be his followers. If you have the smallest grasp of redemptive history as it runs through the Bible, you will understand that God the Father is about "gracious choosing." He chooses his people out of his great heart of love, not based upon anything special in them (Deut 7:7–9; 10:14–16). And Jesus told his twelve disciples, "You did not choose me, but I chose you and appointed you that you should go and bear fruit and that your fruit should abide, so that whatever you ask the Father in my name, he may give it to you" (John 15:16).

Using wisdom and insight (that he will willingly grant to us as well), Jesus chose twelve men to be his closest followers and out of those, he chose three to whom he gave what we might call special or more intimate

---

4. I only met with *men* on an individual basis as a church pastor.

preference. Dr. Coleman writes, ". . . the more concentrated the size of the group being taught, the greater opportunity for effective instruction."[5] Jesus's strategy was to make a large impact on a small number of chosen men. Yes, as Coleman points out in chapter 1 of his book, Jesus did not neglect the masses. "In every way possible Jesus manifested to the masses of humanity a genuine concern. These were the people that He came to save – he loved them, wept over them, and finally died to save them from their sin. No one could think that Jesus shirked mass evangelism."[6] Apparently, small group and one-on-one ministry can be done without completely sacrificing the larger community.

Realistically speaking, this concept of selection always gives pause to those for whom I suggest it. A natural cascade of questions comes to mind: "Won't I be accused of favoritism?" "Is it not fair to invest in some and neglect others?" "How can you leave, or choose to leave, someone else out of your strategy?" "Won't your neglect of others appear insensitive?" "Shouldn't the pastor/leader/discipler try to invest equally in everyone?" "Won't you be subject to the accusation that you are forming a clique?" And my first answer is always, "Yes, all of these questions are fair to ask." On the other hand, I must add that these questions will not appear at all if you do not agree with Coleman's premise (or what appears to be Jesus's strategy for training men). You will simply minister indiscriminately (if that is truly possible) to everyone, while potentially focusing upon no one. Philosophically, I am not sure that strategy will make you a leader of men (or women), nor will it help you in building Christ's vision for the church and its future. *The Master Plan of Evangelism* strategy is about investing in present and future leaders of the church, an effort that does not involve everyone in the ministry or group. The alternative is maintenance, i.e., the goal of keeping everything going as it is, or maintaining the status quo of the group or organization. I think that the alternative philosophy of ministering to everyone equally is impossible. No one person can conceivably minister to the large group (the masses) while simultaneously meeting everyone's needs; that goal is not conceivable nor attainable.

Everyone interested in ministering to others becomes selective about those to whom they give themselves, their time, and their effort. And this selectivity includes choosing! When I led the RUF ministry at the University of Florida, my group was never huge. I'm not sure I would say that

---

5. Ibid., 27.
6. Ibid., 28.

it was even large. But one year I did have a core group of student leaders made up of twelve male and female students, somewhat indicative of the growth in our group. Having worked with much smaller leadership groups in the past, reaching the "biblical" number of twelve appeared to be a landmark achievement. I also had three RUF interns (college graduates who spend two or three years working with college students) at one point, although that number lasted only briefly. With 36,000 students attending the University of Florida at that time (probably 23,000 in the undergraduate program) and another 10,000 students attending Sante Fe Community College in Gainesville, where should I place my focus? It is obvious that God had raised up a handful of students out of that enormous number, students whom he had entrusted into my hands. How many students were actually involved in my RUF ministry on campus? In some ways, I never knew. Our large group meeting was small. But there were students who attended small group Bible studies who didn't attend the large group. And there were students with whom RUF students and I were engaging in one-on-one contexts who were not attending the large group or small group meetings. It really didn't matter if they attended our meetings (of course we wanted them to do so); these students could be considered at the least as "fringe members" of the ministry, since our students were ministering to them. We had no official membership or roll, so if you asked these fringe students if they were a part of RUF, they might actually answer either way, yes or no.

So, the question for me regarding the campus was, "To whom or into whom do I place my life, time, effort, and energies?" Based on *The Master Plan of Evangelism*, I chose to spend the bulk of my time meeting with my core group (key) leaders as well as with my interns. And I have no regrets for doing so. Again, Coleman writes,

> Jesus was a realist. He fully realized the fickleness of depraved human nature as well as the Satanic forces of this world amassed against humanity, and in this knowledge He based His evangelism on a plan that would meet the need. The multitudes of discordant and bewildered souls were potentially ready to follow Him, but Jesus individually could not possibly give them the personal care they needed. His only hope was to get men imbued with His life who would do it for Him. Hence, He concentrated Himself upon those who were to be the beginning of this leadership. Though He did what He could to help the multitudes, He had to devote Himself primarily to a few men, rather than the masses, in order

that the masses could at last be saved. This was the genius of His strategy.[7]

My second priority lay in the category of potential or rising leadership, although new or non-Christian students were definitely a passion of mine. Our group was small enough, however, that I believe I could say that all of the "members" of the group knew that I was interested in them and their well-being. I was a pastor to our students, although pastoral ministry, as well as counseling others, is not my strength. This commitment to spend time with student leaders, interns, rising leaders, and "outsiders" (possibly non-Christians) was premised on other philosophical statements made by Dr. Coleman in *The Master Plan of Evangelism*. He submits, in his chapter on Delegation, "Jesus was always building up in His ministry to the time when His disciples would have to take over His work, and go out into the world with the redeeming Gospel."[8]

Furthermore, when Coleman discusses the topic of reproduction, he states, "It did not matter how small the group was to start with so long as they reproduced and taught their disciples to reproduce."[9] As a campus minister, I wasn't necessarily going anywhere, i.e., leaving these students (and in reality, I would watch this core group of twelve students graduate and leave college), but I hoped that by investing in them, they would continue to do kingdom work wherever they moved.

So, I became fully committed to the leaders in the group, believing that if I invested in them, their growth in Christ and passion for him and his kingdom would overflow to the other college students being reached by our ministry. I never ignored any students in our ministry but I had to be selective in my focus; therefore, I gave that special attention to my student leaders. I was following the principle that Jesus used, which is a philosophical one—I prioritized the leaders and possible future leaders in my campus ministry. This meant that I met with them every other week or so and sometimes weekly (at their request) to do Bible study, training, to discuss their lives, progress and problems, and to see how they were doing in the ministry efforts in which they were engaged. We also had weekly core group (leadership) meetings, usually at our home when possible, and core group retreats (planning, training, and strategy). I would surmise that probably almost every campus ministry that exists functions somewhat

7. Ibid., 33.
8. Ibid., 82.
9. Ibid., 106.

in this manner, although as an ordained minister, I was a true pastor to students (in essence, maybe not in function), and my goal was to assist the students to learn to lead. Whatever they learned in our campus ministry was designed to help them serve Christ's church, wherever they would wind up settling.

Criteria for Selection

How did I select the students with whom I worked? I would like to say "natural selection," but that doesn't sound too good! Much of the choosing was natural however, and based on the use of sanctified common sense. I definitely looked for students in whom God was obviously working, those who were growing in the Lord or at least willing to learn and be taught. I usually became interested in them and their potential because I had observed how they responded to God's Word in their own lives. I looked for relational chemistry, i.e., students who related well to me, as well as to others. I wanted students who were willing to function in a group setting and as a group member. I looked for humility, even if the student was feisty (I usually like feisty). I looked for those who were sensitive to the Lord's will. This attribute was crucial. I myself am a skeptic and battle cynicism and know that such an attitude can be debilitating in a team context. But the desire to ultimately do the Lord's will, no matter what he requires, is a picture of a person submitted to the Lordship of Christ.[10]

Association

I looked for students who were mature enough to want the group's well-being as much as their own; that quality takes time to develop but it can happen rather quickly in a college environment. I did not necessarily look for natural leaders because I knew (from Dr. Coleman) that Jesus chose his followers based on their future potential, not their present offering or assessment. Ultimately, as Dr. Coleman states in chapter 2 of *The Master Plan of Evangelism*, I chose these students, just as Jesus chose his disciples, "to be with them."[11] Coleman writes, in the first sentence from his chapter

---

10. Unlike most adults, serious Christian college students of this sort can be abused by authoritative types; it is a crime against God when that happens. I tried to never manipulate or abuse students with my role of authority.

11. cf. Mark 3:14; Luke 6:13.

entitled Association, "Having called His men, Jesus made it a practice to be with them. This was the essence of His training program – just letting His disciples follow Him."[12] I must candidly say that I enjoyed being with and associating with all of my student leaders (yes, some were more challenging than others), and I was able to get to know them well. Association is one of the great joys in the life of the disciple investor.

Again, I write this about campus ministry because although it is more challenging to accomplish in the local church, I do believe that this philosophy of selection and association can be applied within the framework of the local church. The pastor and even the layperson can implement a focus on a few with the hope for growth in both personal sanctification and maturity in the lives of his disciples, with a goal of future reproduction. As a matter of fact, I believe that church revitalization can occur with this strategy, if the pastor has enough time to invest in the church's future *and* if he remains in place for the long haul. The general principle to follow and the question to ask is, "With whom do I spend my time with the hopes that they will become more Christ-like and more effective servant-leaders in my church?" The answer to that question could very well determine both the future and vitality of your church. And if you can get some laypeople to buy into the concept enough to get involved, who knows what might happen!

In Church Planting

Criteria for Selection

Moving to the topic of the church plant, where do we start? In campus ministry, I had both new students and potential leaders in need of development *arriving every year*, if not every semester. It was essential that I be assertive (or aggressive) enough to go after them, meet with them, and begin the diagnosis process in their lives. However, in my church planting experience, everyone, in some way, was new to the church because the church was new. Yet many had been "invested in" somewhere and somehow in the past (whether for good or bad), so they were not necessarily new in the faith or to church life. Some were obvious leaders, having led in the past (and having been ordained as ruling elders or deacons), but I still needed to get to know them in order to discover the following:

---

12. Ibid., 38.

- Do they presently love the Lord, his church, and are they seeking to be godly or Christ-like? Is this true for their spouses as well? Are both husband and wife seeking to know the Lord better and together? In what ways?
- Are they on board with what we are hoping to do as a new church? (i.e., do they support the philosophy of ministry that I espouse as church planter?)
- Are they with me and will they support me as their leader in this new work? (This is a very crucial question.)
- Do we share similar theological convictions, commitments, and confessions of faith?
- Who are they? Do we have enough chemistry to work together as a mutually supportive team? Do we like each other and can we trust each other? (Trust is huge.)
- Where do their spouses (and/or children) fit into what we are trying to do? Are the spouses supportive of the work?

If the answers to all of the above questions were positive enough so that it appeared we could work together to build Christ's church in a *church planting* setting, then these were the individuals I would choose to help lead the work, i.e., these were those specific people in whom I would invest myself, my time, my effort, and my energy. It must be understood that, firstly, my theological tradition ordains men only, so I am speaking in the male context.[13]

Secondly, though as a church planter I had some freedom to find, recruit, and train my future leaders, ultimately these leaders would be examined by a presbytery examinations committee created for the sole purpose of assuring quality control. This examinations committee would exercise that quality control in two particular areas: personal godliness (more difficult for outsiders to assess), and theological conformity to our church's standards (easier to assess). Thirdly, before these men could become ordained or installed officers (ruling elders or deacons) in the local church plant, I would require them to attend and be trained through a

---

13. I might add that I could be comfortable working with women serving in non-ordained leadership capacities, if my situation were to require it. In my case, in two church plants, my focus was primarily on male leadership, but also included their spouses as a priority.

thorough twelve week officer training course (I also included the wives, if willing, and they usually were). I would personally choose those whom I would like to have attend the training. This also meant that I would try to diplomatically discourage those who were not ready or were seemingly not fit for the office, including those whom I knew might not fully support me personally or philosophically. Then during, or immediately after, the officer's training (this happens in churches all the time, particularly church plants), some of the men I chose would drop out of their pursuit of the office, due to either having counted the cost of serving, having experienced providential circumstances that prevented them from serving, or having been personally discouraged by myself or others from pursuing the leadership position at that time.

I must add that this selection and association process occurs all along the way in the life of the church plant. A church planter has a pool of men in the congregation and from that pool (one that I discovered is growing and changing all the time) the church planter is progressively choosing those with whom he wants to spend personal time as he tries to discern whether these men could be future leaders of the church. In reality, in my case it meant that I originally started spending time with a lot of men, if not the majority of them, on an individual basis. (Remember, in a church plant there usually are not that many men.) Then as I got to know and diagnose them, looking for answers to the six questions listed above, I began to cull the list so that I could focus on those who were potential leaders with whom I could work. These men became those with whom I intentionally chose to spend time in order to discern whether I wanted to invest increasingly more time in them. Thus, I moved from selection to association. In reality, I have just described a philosophy of disciple investing (and leadership recruiting/training) that not all ministers or church leaders will necessarily agree with or implement. In finding church leaders, I wanted to choose discerningly and associate strategically. I would call this process "leadership development" and I believe most ministers do try to develop leaders. At least I hope they do; therefore, this philosophy is certainly one leadership training plan to consider.

In the Established Church

I would now like to consider disciple investing in the established church, i.e., not in the context of a church plant. Working in an established church has not been my experience from a leadership standpoint. However, I have attended a few of them and have observed not only churches but also pastors who served established congregations in my denomination. The challenge of the established church is that frequently the leaders are not only established but have served in their respective roles for a long time. Some might be described as entrenched. Nevertheless, the pastor who wishes to see an established church changed or revitalized would do well to focus upon the present leaders, as well as potential future leaders. If he can commit himself toward remaining at the church for a long time, he can use a healthy strategy that aims at discipling new and upcoming leaders and incorporating them into the present leadership structure.

Discovering New Leaders

Potential or possible new leaders rise to the surface in a number of ways:

1. Conversion—leading people to the Lord, helping them grow in Christ, and watching and waiting for them to become mature members. This approach certainly requires a commitment for the long haul for the pastor of a congregation. Yet, if people are coming to know the Lord and the pastor is involved in their conversions or their growth, even the most staid and established church will be an exciting place to be!

2. Helping young, untaught believers grow, maybe for the first time ever—every church has people like this among their congregation. The question is whether or not these members (or regular attendees) truly want to grow. If they do, the experience is almost as rewarding as watching a new convert grow. The growth of a long-time believer who has never been stimulated to use the means of grace can resemble a small struggling plant that simply needs a larger planting pot and some fertilizer. The resulting changes can be staggering.

3. Focusing upon and working with rising leadership—believers who, for whatever reason, have not been recruited, "enlisted" in the cause or ministries of the church, developed, encouraged, or trained. Whether due to personal insecurity, intimidation by present leadership, a lack of confidence in the individual by the ruling leadership, or simply a lack of exposure in the use of gifts and skills, this person is sitting on the sidelines but shouldn't be. The rising leader may be a "sleeper" (quiet and behind the scenes but potentially gifted) or an unknown.

Yet if the pastor will take special time to invest in this person, he can raise up someone who will become a new leader, as well as an individual who is usually guaranteed to support the pastor's vision and ministry.

4. Working closely with a teachable leader who is presently serving or has served in the past—some leaders have never been truly discipled, taught or led by someone who really cares about their spiritual nurture. The flower is ready to bloom but the nurture has never been provided. Again, this commitment takes time and lots of intentional input but it is well worth the effort.

5. Working with a present leader who simply needs to build a trustworthy relationship with a pastor, such as he has never known—some leaders have been "burned" in their past relationships with previous pastoral staff. For whatever reason (disrespect, manipulation, conflict), this leader will not work as a teammate with the pastor or possible other leaders. If this person becomes a contrarian or an adversary to the pastor, it will be almost impossible to win him over. However, if the relationship is not purely adversarial, there is hope that through a serious relationship building process, the leader can develop into one who holds a supportive role in the future of the ministry. In essence, this person becomes a "new" leader in the ministry.

Again, in the established church, the pastor/leader must decide if a special focus on leadership training will be the emphasis of his ministry. He must decide if this will be the priority that drives his time and forms his schedule. This selection and association process will likely determine both the future of the church and his ministry. Will he give extra time to leadership development? Such a decision appears to sacrifice time given to the ministry and members at large. Will he make an added effort to spend time with his future key leaders? Will he clear his schedule of secondary ministry commitments to personally see these future leaders on a regular basis? Can he learn to say no to ministry distractions, i.e., reading an unnecessary book, spending time watching that extra television program or playing that video game, or spending time with the person who shows up only to waste his time? Can he turn his attention and efforts to this most joyous (and yet difficult) aspect of the ministry, which is loving others into the image of Christ-like leadership? Dr. Coleman is correct in his previously mentioned quote when he says, "Seen in this way, though, it becomes a big decision in ministry. One must decide where he wants his ministry to count – in the momentary applause of popular recognition or in the reproduction of his life in a few chosen men who will carry on his work after he has gone."[14]

Working it Out

There will be some leaders who cannot conceive of this approach to ministry, i.e., they do not buy into Robert Coleman's assessment of Christ's disciple making plan. I do not fault them. Some love pastoral ministry so much that a focus primarily on leadership development does not, or cannot, appeal to them. Such a leader is a pastor-teacher who thrives on the caring (priestly) aspect of the ministry and loves to be with every member of the body of Christ, sharing both their joys and their sorrows. *Presence* is a superior value for this leader, and being with the flock as much as possible is his passion. Some leaders are not inclined toward the mentoring aspect of ministry simply because it is not part of their disposition or inclination. Others are not skilled or gifted in the area of delegation (another chapter in *The Master Plan of Evangelism*) and hence are not able to let go of certain compelling duties or responsibilities. Whether it is a matter of control or conscientiousness, they like or want to do most everything. Others still may lack the constitution necessary to strategically implement a leadership development plan, or the time management skills needed to pull off the necessary "weekly life structure" of managing intentional meetings with future leaders. These reasons for not pursuing a "master plan of evangelism" strategy, such as Coleman describes, are providentially legitimate in my view. I've seen a lot of ministry and met with and viewed many ministers over the years, essentially throughout my entire life, and I would never prescribe a one-size-fits-all mentality for carrying forth the ministry and calling of pastoring a church.

A Legitimate Working Model

Nevertheless, what I am suggesting is that whether or not we are addressing ministry on the campus, in the church plant, or in the established church, the philosophy of ministry espoused by *The Master Plan of Evangelism* does provide a legitimate, working model for carrying forth that ministry. In

14. Ibid., 37.

other words, this strategic approach to ministry can be practically executed in most any ministry setting. The pastor/leaders must decide how they are going to use their time. They must decide upon whom they will focus their attention. As mentioned above, while in campus ministry I would make easily ten one-on-one appointments with students each week during a busy semester. Sometimes I would schedule 12–15 appointments, including meals. I thrived on these personal opportunities. Of these appointments, probably three or four were primarily focused on present leaders (core group members) or campus interns each week. I believed (and still do) that my time with these key leaders in the ministry would trickle down and multiply as they took my teaching, training, guidance, and support and passed it along to others in campus ministry. The campus constantly surfaces rising leadership. Therefore, the campus minister or staff person must continually be sensitive and watch for those possible, future leaders necessary to carry on the work. Otherwise the ministry will suffer in both the short and the long term.

Similarly, the church plant must normally surface leaders committed to the cause in order to survive. The church planter must work with experienced leaders who join the work or else he must find and develop the rising and future leaders. This responsibility is often one of the harsh challenges of making a church plant (organism) into a functioning church (organization). As previously mentioned, finding the time to invest in these possible leaders is more difficult to do. Thus, the leader/pastor must be fully committed to the worthiness of this effort and prioritize it in his life and ministry. On top of this, he will have extra responsibilities that are generic to working within a church plant setting (networking, promotional skills, administration, etc., that established churches usually already have by the very nature of their organizational longevity).

Therefore, whereas I could make 10–15 personal appointments per week with college students, I found it very difficult to make more than five or six of these appointments in the church planting context. I attempted to see at least one potential or present leader each week but unlike campus ministry, I never met with any particular leader every week on a regular basis for any duration of time. Such an action seemed almost impossible. Moreover, I am not sure if these individuals would have valued that effort or even have had the time to meet with such regularity. Nevertheless, once the church plant became organized, I made it my priority to meet with my five ruling elders individually on a regular basis for the purposes of relationship building (friendship and trust), conflict management (or conflict prevention through regular communication), shepherding discussion, vision casting, and fostering unity. In addition to these meetings, I tried to make appointments with recent visitors, responsive people (those who appeared to be growing in Christ, yet whom I did not know very well), and potential rising leadership (strategic meetings). I loved meeting with new people, as it was a natural passion, with evangelism in mind.

Delegating to Leaders

This method of ministry, however, was predicated on one key facet: I expected my leaders to be shepherds and to assist me in watching over the flock. I groomed my men to do this task, whether they were overly gifted for it or not. In some ways, without explaining it to them, I had to convince them to apply the principles of *The Master Plan of Evangelism* into their own lives. I would associate with them, impart to them what I could, demonstrate ministry when I could, and delegate to them. Of course, I learned plenty from them as well. And having spent considerable time with them prior to their examination as officers of the church, I already knew that these men were "consecrated." The key to this method of ministry was the delegation aspect: how was I going to make one-on-one meetings a priority in my own ministry schedule? The only way possible was for me to ask my ruling elders not only to oversee the church as an organization but to oversee the souls and lives of the people. Therefore, once the church was organized and these men were placed into the office of ruling elder, I immediately assigned them families and individuals whom they would shepherd.

This ministry of elder shepherding assisted me in freeing up some of my time, time that usually would have been spent in the ministry of caretaking. It also enabled me not only to schedule appointments with my shepherding elders (for the purposes mentioned above), but to visit and meet with new visitors to the church, to follow up with people going through the membership classes, and to work with potential rising or new leadership. Eventually, the church hired a second staff person, a very valuable older seminary student who became my pastoral assistant while he trekked through his seminary training. He and his wife (who was also very committed to doing ministry) became a priority for my individual attention as well. I definitely found my ministry exponentially increased due to this couple's many gifts and labors! I appreciate them to this day and whatever investment I made in their lives was, without question, fully returned to bless my ministry and life as a pastor.

Because my ruling elders were helping me with pastoral needs, counseling, mercy ministry, and crisis management, my personal ministry of disciple investing (though more limited than it was in campus ministry) could thrive. Although I continued to maintain the pastoral responsibility of overseeing *all* the "souls" of the congregation (we weren't that large— around 160 adults and children combined, and I knew them all), I delegated some of that responsibility out, thus freeing up my schedule to some extent. I valued every extra hour for disciple investing that I gained from this strategy. I believe the elders themselves would say that they enjoyed their shepherding responsibilities on the whole. Some admittedly were better than others at the task, but they all equally embraced the opportunity. Furthermore, the people (the sheep) seemed to understand the philosophy behind the method as well (I did explain it in the new members' or Inquirers' class). No one ever told me I wasn't doing enough for them. (Of course, some did want me to visit more and I can't blame them for that; I tried to respond to those, though they were a small minority.) Yet, on the positive side, others commented that they didn't know elders could be so pastoral (I was blessed to have some very good pastoral elders). I had just five elders but that was enough for a congregation of our size.

I explain all of this not to say that my plan was a roaring success (although it did work pretty well), but simply to say that one-on-one disciple investing can happen as a normal and regular part of a pastor's or leader's ministry. Delegation and the letting go of certain responsibilities and expectations is a key element in making this happen. I had to sell both my elders (in officers' training) and my people (in the membership or "Inquirers'" class) on the concept. I am not sure that all were convinced, but on the whole the method functioned very well. In some ways, my pastoral survival was predicated on it. I needed help to do pastoral ministry even for a group of under 200 people. I was forced to learn to delegate better, a skill that grew during my campus ministry years, but one that still remained a weakness in my life. Thankfully my leaders were willing to comply and participate to the best of their abilities.

Shepherding the Flock

As for the process of helping shepherding elders actually shepherd the flock, I oversaw this on a monthly basis at our regular session (elder) meetings. As a matter of fact, shepherding the flock was probably the priority task of those meetings. I would, of course, hear about various personal needs in between these meetings (sometimes on a daily basis) and was aware of the struggles and problems that stem from the nature of crises and other problems that surface before the pastor. But the first line of pastoral support was designed to be (theoretically) the shepherding elder, as long as he was staying in touch with his sheep as he ought. The second line of support (and one that allowed me more opportunities for one-on-one appointments) was the creation of small groups. These small groups were called "Care Groups." I debated over this label because I was a bit concerned about the reputation of the feminization of the church among unbelievers, and "Care Groups" didn't sound very masculine. But I wanted and hoped that this small group ministry would be characterized by life-on-life sharing, prayer, support, and *care* for one another. If the people or members of the church would think in terms of caring for one another's needs, as opposed to viewing that role as solely the pastoral staff's responsibility, then this would further enable me to focus on my desire to do personal disciple investing. As you can see, I was giving away some pastoral opportunities to both my leaders and my members. I think that everyone benefits from this blueprint of local church ministry.

The bottom line to this strategy is to find time to meet with your leaders individually while in the busyness of ministry. If a pastor spends 12–20 hours per week in sermon preparation, he then has about 30–40 plus hours to accomplish other ministry tasks (and we know that the pastor's work is, in reality, never done). Somehow the pastor/leader must set times for meeting with leaders, rising leaders and potential leaders if he wants to be involved in the personal realm of disciple investing. He cannot succeed in this goal if he is constantly taking care of every member's pastoral needs. On the other hand, church work can be done and the church can continue on without pastoral disciple investing occurring. But my view is that maintaining church life without investing in specific, key potential-laden individuals is a sad way to do ministry because the pastor misses out on the joys of investing in and sharing the discipling process. Making time for disciple investing is a sure means to pastoral encouragement in the midst of a job that often deals with a lot of discouragement.

Disciple Investing Methods

Finally, I would like to mention just a handful of observations of how I have seen disciple investing occur in real-life situations. In these instances, I am going to remind the reader of the three avenues of ministry or disciple investing. Those are one-on-one, small group, and large group ministry. Each of these avenues provide a context where Christ disciples his followers and changes their lives. Preaching in worship and teaching in Sunday School or other settings is large group disciple investing. Small group Bible discussion, prayer, service, or ministry is a form of disciple investing. And of course, I hope I have built my case for one-on-one disciple investing without suggesting that it is the only or even the best method. However, I do like it a lot.

What I am about to share is a brief summary of a handful of disciple investing methods I have seen work. The first is what I term "large group" disciple investing. It could also be termed a programmatic method. On occasion, I have seen a church and its leaders decide that a certain year will be "The Year for Discipleship!" in the church. Sometimes this program promotes itself using the theme, "Every Member a Disciple." In this plan, the church makes a concerted effort to try and find a comprehensive curriculum that covers a vast span of age groups. The goal is for everyone (members and regular attendees with no age limit) to walk through the same curriculum. Though a task this large is very challenging, I have seen this ambitious goal function through some easier, more manageable methods. Those methods are:

Large Group Disciple Investing—Working it Out

Everyone reads through the Bible in a year (or two years) in a planned manner as families or individuals. The church presents a system of Bible reading based on the calendar year(s) to everyone involved in the church's ministry with hopes that everyone will at least read more of the Bible than ever before (recognizing the reality that some of the participants may not actually read the entire Bible through.) Sermons, small groups, or Sunday School classes might address a portion of the passages assigned and read during the respective week.

Everyone is expected (or encouraged) to memorize key Scripture verses throughout the year, using a uniform selection of verses. The church might present these verses as weekly or monthly goals (i.e., a verse per week/month), with the key verse made into a banner to be draped in some prominent area(s) of the church, or splashed weekly in the church bulletin (or e-newsletter or some other type of church wide communication.) Some churches put the banners up in the sanctuary, while others place them in Sunday School rooms, in the fellowship hall, or in all of the above suggested locations.

The Navigators' Colossians 2:7 Series is a program that was founded with something like "mass discipleship" in mind, although it was often implemented in a small group format with hopes for large group involvement. However, the *Colossians 2:7* format proved to be too overwhelming (in particular, too long) for large-scale acceptance and for individual completion. Despite its weaknesses I believe that, as far as discipleship programs go, the creation of the *Colossians 2:7* series was, at the time, a valiant effort to help people move forward in their walks with Christ and can still be helpful in that stated endeavor.

Small Group Disciple Investing—Working it Out

In considering "small group" disciple investing, I have watched from a distance the methods used by two evangelical Presbyterian pastors who are truly leaders and disciplers of men in their own right. Both men have pastored very large churches (megachurches) and yet have maintained the priority and ability to invest in future leaders.

The first example I would like to cite is Dr. Harry Reeder, a man who has pastored both Christ Covenant PCA Church in Charlotte, North Carolina, and Briarwood PCA Church in Birmingham, Alabama. Both churches have had thousands of members. The following is the simplest description of his disciple investing ministry that I can write, since what I know is what I have heard and seen from a distance.

When ministering in Charlotte, Dr. Reeder constantly developed church leaders and future church leaders. He used a method that he learned from a fellow minister in the Miami area, Dr. Terry Gyger. Being mentored by Dr. Gyger, Dr. Reeder in turn mentored other men. He simply ministered to men at Christ Covenant through daily (and weekly) early morning small group meetings of accountability and primarily Bible study. He would gather together separate groups of 8–12 men four mornings a week, prior to the workday hours. Through his leadership, these men would pray together, share, and study Scripture. In order to simplify his preparation, he used the same material for all groups. He also did a similar lunch study two times each week. It is probably impossible to count the men in whom Dr. Reeder invested in this manner. He tried to go to bed early every evening in order to maintain this morning schedule. Such investing was obviously a priority to him and an effective methodology for him. It enabled him to invest in scores of men, as one can see by simply doing the math.

I use Dr. Reeder's example to note that any pastor with a commitment to invest in Christ's disciples can use this strategy, even if it were only with three or four men (the more the better, however) and just one morning a week. If you cannot find three to four hours (individual time blocks) during the week to invest individually with your leaders, potential leaders, rising leaders and other men, then choose one morning and engage in small group disciple investing. The freedom of methodology is yours. Small group disciple investing on the part of the pastor or church leader can work in a small church or in a large church. As for myself, as I have alluded to throughout this book, I love one-on-one over small groups but certainly enjoy the dynamics of the small group setting. I should further note that, by observation only, Dr. Reeder gave his ordained and hired staff extra attention as well. It appears to me that, while ministering to a few thousand people, Dr. Reeder was also able to find and make the time to invest in the smaller, influential members of his ministry team. Granted, he had staff and pastors whose job descriptions were to take care of some of the duties that a pastor in a small church might have to take care of himself. However, it must be stated that Dr. Reeder loved to develop men and watch the Lord raise them up for service. Often those men were the ones he hired, from within the church, to fill positions of leadership. These hires were not difficult, such as hiring a church outsider for an open position might be, because he not only already knew them, but also had grown to both love and trust them. Such is the blessing of disciple investing when done by the pastor himself.

Another pastor that I have observed from a distance, over the span of thirty plus years is Randy Pope, the founder and pastor of Perimeter Church in Atlanta. I have already mentioned his definition of discipleship in chapter 1. Randy Pope has developed what he calls "Life-on-Life Missional Discipleship." Rather than try to explain it here, I will simply quote from his website: "Life-on-life Missional Discipleship is a gospel transformation process which involves a mature and equipped follower of Christ (a Discipleship Team Leader) intentionally and relationally investing in others in the context of small groups of four to six people (a Discipleship Team)."[15] The reader can research this method further as desired, but my main point is that Randy Pope started his church with discipleship in mind, and has designed his ministry with a focus on individual men whom he both evangelizes and disciples. He, like Harry Reeder, gives special attention to a specific number of men, as well as to his ministerial staff. "Life on Life Missional Discipleship" is a small group emphasis on disciple investing that flows out of the heart of a pastor who bleeds discipleship.

Although this disciple investing ministry appears programmatic, the explanation of the Perimeter approach is stated thusly,

> Life-on-life discipleship is not curriculum-on-life. We believe that discipleship happens because of relationships, not because of books or materials. There is something organic that takes place in discipleship groups that are healthy even as one works through engineered (i.e., curriculum) content. Although there is a learning component to discipleship, the focus is on living and sharing truth, not merely learning it. Thus, *The Journey* is designed to support a life-on-life process of growth, not a curriculum-on-life process.[16]

The goal, much like that described in Coleman's *The Master Plan of Evangelism*, is to help participants become more like Jesus and know him better through relationships and an organic effort, as opposed to sheer adherence to a curriculum or a specific program. The lesson a pastor can learn from the Perimeter Model is that he can intentionally spend time with individuals and/or small groups of men and give them his life, while pointing them to Christ. Out of this style of pastoral ministry, a church culture or ethos can be formed. Ultimately, the pastor sets the stage for this culture, while protecting and maintaining the vision. Small group disciple investing can become the fruit of and the method for church vitality when it is based on Christ as the source for change and life.

Lastly, I would like to refer to Mr. Pat Morley's book, *No Man Left Behind: How to Build and Sustain a Thriving, Disciple-Making Ministry for Every Man in Your Church*. Mr. Morley's book explains a plan for disciple investing based upon a large group emphasis that includes small group interaction. Using a "gathering" philosophy, men come together in a breakfast setting in the early, pre-work hours, where they hear a presentation

---

15. Pope, "What is Discipleship?"
16. Pope, "Life on Life Journey Curriculum."

by a speaker (or expert) based on topics treated from a biblical perspective. The presentation or message lasts approximately twenty minutes and then the men, sitting in a natural small group structure created by their breakfast table setting, hold open discussions about the topic. Each table has a leader who comes prepared to guide the discussion. These breakfast gatherings may be held on any weekday or Saturday morning. A nucleus of men commits itself to attending the meetings and to inviting other men. The bonding of the men and the relevant topics maintain the momentum, though there must always be some intentional driving force behind the meetings, leaders, and men attending. A disciple investing ministry like this one could be used in a local church or by a parachurch-type ministry created to reach men. It could also be run completely by laypeople (and be developed for women as well, I'm sure). The simplicity of this method is both intriguing and a very useful approach for investing in male disciples in particular.

Involved Layperson

If you are a layperson who has persevered through this book or are reading only this chapter, I would like to say that you can implement many of the ideas contained in this chapter yourself. Depending (of course) upon your training, experience, and Bible knowledge, there are plenty of ways that you personally can invest in disciples. The easiest way is to simply find a person who knows less than you do and tell them more. You may recall the story about my college roommate who became a Christian in our dorm room entering the kingdom of God before my very eyes (and he remembers it very well). All I did, as a young Christian discipling a younger Christian, was purchase him a readable Bible and give him a handful of important Scripture verses to look up and read. Within a few hours, he had finished. Disciple investing can start that simply and easily. You can lead a small group to investigate what the Bible says. It is best to do a lot of study prior to and in preparation for each small group meeting, but you yourself can grow while group members grow as well. You could ask your pastor or the person in charge of Christian education at your church if you can teach a Sunday School class—usually at every church in America, the seventh grade middle school boys' class has an opening! (Just kidding!) You have to start somewhere. At the church I attended in the 1980s, a ruling elder, who was one of the kindest and gentlest men you would ever meet, taught the two year old's Sunday School class for years. He was a man in his fifties at the time and I am quite certain that he taught three of my four children in that context. He was a disciple investor!

You might also build a relationship with a non-Christian and use some diagnostic questions. Based on the answers, if you don't know the Scriptures to reference, go back and study them for yourself. Match the scriptural answers with the questions. This is what Pastor Randy Pope does and much of his discussion deals with basic questions of Christian faith. You can also give a short, readable piece of literature (pamphlet length) on a given topic and say that you would like to get together and discuss it while you're just hanging out together. (I suggest that you buy them a meal and ask the church to pay for it—if the church won't pay for that ministry, they are thinking shortsightedly about Christ's kingdom.) Ask the pastor or a church leader if you can tag along for most any ministry with which you are not familiar. If the pastor is doing hospital visitation, you can learn how to visit from him. Prison ministry? Go for it! Ask your pastor for tips on how to study the Bible better or how to prepare Bible studies better. Ask your pastor how to lead a group or whether you can be mentored by a leader in a small group run by the church. Befriend your neighbor and see what happens. Ask a leader if she can tell you everything she knows. Will this individual meet with you for a few weeks and disciple invest in you? Hang out with the youth group if it's not too awkward for either party. Adopt a young person needing a parent or grandparent figure in his/her life. Prayerfully take the initiative to get involved; share your life, both joys and sorrows, and be real. Be constrained by the love of Christ and do ministry for someone in need of what you have to offer, whether it be a listening ear, a trip to get an ice cream cone, or your quiet bedside presence in the midst of a health crisis. Simply stated, give yourself to another person or other people, and point them to Scripture and to Christ. You will be blessed by doing so!

I close this chapter by simply asking this poignant question: "What is your philosophy of ministry for discipleship, disciple making, disciple building, or disciple investing?" I don't really care what you call it, but what are you doing? Whether you are a pastor, a campus or church staff worker, or other parachurch worker, or a layperson, how are you investing your life in others so that they are growing in Christ-likeness and learning from, following, and loving their master and savior more and more? Listen to the call of Christ. He is still calling you to follow him and he will make you a fisher of men and women. Christ is still changing lives.

Conclusion

Christ is Still Changing Lives!

Jesus: Still Calling and Discipling

When Jesus called his first disciples, as recorded in Matthew chapter 4, he began a ministry which he knew consisted of building his kingdom through a handful of men. "And he said to them, 'Follow me, and I will make you fishers of men.' 20 Immediately they left their nets and followed him" (4:19–20). Two thousand years later, Jesus is still the one who calls his followers everywhere and at every time and when called, every true follower hears the summons of the master as powerfully as those two early disciples, Peter and Andrew. The follower of Jesus is known by the very familiar designation, "disciple." Jesus's kingdom is built and expanded by the process commonly called "discipleship." I have tried to build a case for the term "disciple investing." Why disciple investing? Because just as Jesus invested in a chosen few, knowing that in the Father's plan these seemingly inconsequential men could change the world, so each follower of Jesus is similarly called to invest in others. By investing in others' lives, each follower of Christ invests in the building of Christ's kingdom and ultimately invests in the changing of the world through the gospel.

Am I Investing?

So, the question for each of us is, "What role do I play in the disciple investing process that Jesus is doing in the lives of others?" Thankfully, the answer does not require that we flash around some big numbers or impressive statistics, for simply investing in one other person counts in Jesus's eyes. Numbers can be deceptive. Some years ago, RTS Charlotte, where I have served for well over twenty years, invited the original campus administrator, Dr. Gordon Reed, to come and speak to our Tuesday morning worship chapel. In those early days, chapel met in the Carmel Baptist Church youth meeting room (RTS shared the campus with Carmel Baptist Church) which also served as the library. In a makeshift chapel space created by arranging some metal chairs, Dr. Reed returned to the campus he helped start and spoke that morning before some 20–30 students at most. On that particular morning, my wife, Cathy, was able to attend the chapel service with me and we sat together in the front row. Before Dr. Reed spoke, he looked out at what was just a handful of seminary students and faculty gathered together and made a side remark that I will never forget. As a matter of fact, I don't remember the sermon he preached at all, but I will always remember these words: "I learned a long time ago that I could either make a big impact on a small group of people or I could make a small impact on a large group of people." Without saying a word, Cathy and I turned and looked at each other, fully understanding that whether it had been our intention or not, our ministries in both campus ministry and church planting had focused on making (or trying to make) a large impact on a small number of people. In reality, the Lord had designed our efforts to result in what could be termed "smaller ministries" in order that we could give ourselves more fully to the people he brought our way. In all honesty, though I think we wish we had experienced larger numbers (a constant pressure in our culture), I believe that looking back, we have no regrets at the size of any of our ministries. (Later we also worked with a second small church plant in Charlotte that was nothing but—with a few exceptions—an utter delight!) When we consider the relationships that we have built over the years, some surely deeper than others, we are able to cherish each of them.

Disciple Investing

In the simplest of definitions, disciple investing is taking the time to help one person, a small group of people, or an entire church learn about Christ, love him more, become like him, and live for him wholeheartedly. We have learned about disciple investing from the Apostle Paul himself. One principle of disciple investing derived from Paul's letter to the Galatian church includes his commitment to a style that is very closely aligned to a parenting model. He both mothers and fathers his disciples. He both showers affection upon them as a mother and charges them to imitate him (his

Christ-likeness) as their father. And in a spirit of seeming parental exasperation, he explains that disciple investing is characterized by both pain and perplexity. Nevertheless, his purpose of disciple investing is that Christ might be formed in his followers.

Disciple Investing: Multiple Sources

Disciple investing does not happen in a vacuum. Every disciple that has ever lived, with rare exception, has benefitted from three different contributors for growth and maturity. Each of these influences contributes some facet of spiritual development in the disciple. Firstly, Jesus uses his church to help his disciples grow. One's church or denominational affiliation should have at least an indirect bearing, if not a powerful impact, on the spiritual development of that person's theological, biblical, and spiritual understanding. Some traditions are more influential than others, but just as a corporation creates a "trickle down" influence through culture and training, so a church tradition passes along an honored way of life and thinking to its followers or members.

Secondly, the presence of the local church is essential in the life of the Christian disciple. Although some parachurch organizations and other independent-type ministries might downplay the need or importance of the local church, we know that Christ is building his kingdom throughout the world by means of the local church. The local church is without question investing in its members (and regular attendees) through all of its various ministries. And a good Christ-centered and Bible-centered local church will provide an environment of spiritual transformation in the life of its adherents. The church's pastor, its preaching, its practices, and its personality will definitely rub off on the involved disciple.

Finally, the disciple's personal preferences will come to bear on her own growth. The individual's understanding of Scripture, developing (or developed) convictions (right or wrong), and personal experiences in life are all factors that demonstrate the growing disciple's starting point in the maturing process. One's church tradition, local church, and personal preferences all greatly (although not equally) impact the life of the individual disciple of Christ.

Responses to Disciple Investing

Once a person becomes committed to and begins to pursue the ministry of disciple investing, he will encounter various responses from those whom he approaches. Those responses will range from the more difficult attitudes of the respondent, such as resistance or unbelief (non-Christian), or possibly worse, the lukewarm or phony (fake) Christian. There is also the person who is willing to be involved in the disciple investing process but is unsure or intimidated by it. Furthermore, there are those who require some hand-holding, guidance, or personal support and counsel. The more exciting (or seemingly easier) encounters occur with those disciples who are actively growing and maturing in their walks with Christ. And once they do grow and mature, the opportunities abound that assist them in learning how to teach others how to be trained. Eventually, a core group of these aspiring disciples gains the ability to lead others in either the group or the organization, thus becoming leaders who reproduce. Reproduction might be demonstrated in investing in other disciples, raising new leaders, or becoming involved in new ministries that lift up Christ.

In the practice of disciple investing, one of the goals is to help the growing disciple understand how to live all of life in submission to and under the lordship of Jesus Christ. Such a lifestyle only comes to pass properly as the disciple understands the teachings of Scripture while applying the Bible to all of areas of life. The Bible speaks to all questions necessary for living the Christian life in a world that is contrary to holiness. The Apostle Peter writes,

> [3] His divine power has granted to us all things that pertain to life and godliness, through the knowledge of him who called us to his own glory and excellence, [4] by which he has granted to us his precious and very great promises, so that through them you may become partakers of the divine nature, having escaped from the corruption that is in the world because of sinful desire. [5] For this very reason, make every effort to supplement your faith with virtue, and virtue with knowledge, [6] and knowledge with self-control, and self-control with steadfastness, and steadfastness with godliness, [7] and godliness with brotherly affection, and brotherly affection with love. 8 For if these qualities are yours and are increasing, they keep you from being ineffective or unfruitful in the knowledge of our Lord Jesus Christ. [9] For whoever lacks these qualities is so nearsighted that he is blind, having forgotten that he was cleansed from his former sins. [10] Therefore, brothers,

be all the more diligent to confirm your calling and election, for if you practice these qualities you will never fall. ¹¹ For in this way there will be richly provided for you an entrance into the eternal kingdom of our Lord and Savior Jesus Christ.[1]

Scripture Based

Therefore, the disciple investor needs to study the word of God and become familiar with the specific Scripture passages that come to bear on the issues of living out the Christian life. Studying and applying Scripture to life, through the power of the Holy Spirit, is the primary means to becoming more Christ-like. There is little that is more exciting (in all of life, I would contend) than helping another person look at God's word and watching him respond to it in such a way that brings transformation almost right before your eyes. Conversion (being changed in heart, mind, and will by the gospel) and sanctification (responding to God's will through repentance and faith so that one's life is truly changed) are the most exhilarating experiences for a disciple investor to observe. The areas of need in the life of a disciple are usually numerous, so the starting point depends upon the specific needs of the individual disciple. A simple procedure is all that is necessary to begin the ministry of disciple investing:

- Build a Relational Bridge
- Befriend
- Diagnose
- Apply biblical salve/solutions to the point/area(s) of need
- Watch God work!

How blessed you will be to be a part of what God is doing in another's (and your own) life!

Spiritual Diagnosis

In order to minister to others, disciple investors must be "people focused." They therefore will guide their ministry methods by a philosophy of ministry that is committed to discovering and responding to the needs of

---

1. 2 Peter 1: 3–11.

other people. I define this ministry as "spiritual diagnosis," a procedure that focuses upon soul care, such as being a physician of the soul. Diagnosis includes the concept of "pitching and catching," a helpful metaphor for viewing the practice of ministry to others. It includes asking the right questions, constant probing when necessary, listening to answers, and then determining the applicable scriptural prescription (i.e., taking a look at a passage that addresses the needs and issues of the broken soul). Spiritual diagnosis is a process leading to spiritual counsel and guidance based upon the Scriptures. I believe much fruitful ministry arises out of the context of asking questions and attempting to understand people in that manner. What do they think, how do they feel, and how do they act? What background contributed to their thoughts, emotions, and actions? The science of asking questions begins by knowing the right questions to ask, in this case, questions that lend themselves to personal spiritual insight. The art of diagnosis revolves around developing relationships, i.e., building bridges, asking questions, listening and being genuinely interested, and responding. The art also includes taking time to listen to others and knowing when to speak. It includes knowing when to ask questions and what questions are appropriate given the setting and the context of the conversation.

The Three Domains of the Heart

Becoming a follower of Christ requires a true conversion of the heart. I have contended that conversion and heart transformation touch all three domains of the heart: the mind, the emotion, and the will. Our minds must be convinced by the gospel claims, our emotions must be moved by our personal sin against God and the obvious cost of the cross, and our wills must be touched in such a way that behavior changes. Conversion occurs only through the power and work of the Holy Spirit. Similarly, disciple investing must focus upon the sanctification process through an engagement of the mind, an acceptance of expressions of the emotions, and the necessity of repentance and the Christ-like behavior that will naturally flow out of transformed thinking and feeling. Though striving for such a balance in heart transformation is somewhat hypothetical, every believer (and each disciple investor and/or his system) must at least try to avoid an imbalance in any of these domains of the heart. A disciple investor should note the influences of a disciple's church, pastor, and religious heritage or tradition.

Even the disciple investor needs to be aware of their own potential imbalances, while seeking to improve upon notable areas of weakness.

Methods and Models

As we observe the various approaches of disciple investing, we will certainly encounter multiple methods and models designed or utilized for pouring into the lives of Christ's disciples. There is personal discipleship (or personal disciple investing), which is the process of learning to follow Christ through an individual or individuals, normally in a relational context. There is system discipleship, the process of learning to follow Christ through the holistic influence of an organization, whether in and through a church or some other type of ministry context. And there is "at-large disciple investing" which describes the process that occurs when a follower of Christ sits under a variety of Christian influences that intersect with that person's life and consequently changes or impacts her. More common in many ways, but often overlooked, is the method of organic discipleship which is a focus on the spiritual growth of the individual that occurs through the corporate influence of the community of believers, along with all that they have to offer as the body of Christ. Programmatic disciple investing is probably the most utilized method or model. It focuses on the spiritual growth of the individual through a planned and/or structured (programmatic) method of learning, experience, and expectations. There is also the rarest model of disciple investing, the military model, which requires a high demand or regimented layout of performance, including high expectations and strict submission and obedience throughout the prescribed process. We also noted that there are three avenues for disciple investing, each unique and effective in its own way: large group, small group, and one-on-one. Lastly, we emphasized that holistic disciple investing will be exhibited in the three domains mentioned in chapter eight: the cognitive, the affective, and the volitional.

One Last Story

I close by mentioning a story without a known conclusion. As a college student at the University of South Carolina, I was heavily involved in Cru. While serving, I met and ministered to and with a number of students. One student whom I met was a young man from the greater Columbia area; he didn't live on campus but got involved with Cru on a somewhat part time basis. His name was Larry. Larry was a likeable guy, easy going, relatively quiet, and not overly assertive. But his laid back style and warmth made him very approachable, and we would sit and talk at times, never growing overly close to one another. Simply stated, we liked each other, enjoyed our conversations with each other, and were happy to find mutual support while trying to navigate college life as Christians. Eventually we both graduated. I moved on to seminary and as I recall, Larry found a job in the business world in Columbia. A couple of years passed and Larry was forgotten. We had both moved on.

But one day, while visiting the Columbia Mall in the northeast part of town, I ran into Larry. Meeting again was a surprising and positive pleasure for both of us. We engaged in typical small talk, briefly catching up with each other's lives. I was prompted in the conversation to ask Larry about his church. It was an awkward moment. Larry, like a few of my former campus ministry friends, had graduated from college but hadn't managed to find a local church in which to be involved. Graduating "out of" Christian fellowship is hardly an unusual experience for students who finish college. And Larry was no exception. Hearing his circumstances, all I said to Larry was, "Come on Larry, you can't let that happen!" I spoke with an air of incredulity, frustration, and mild displeasure. I don't know if it was one of my finer moments. Thankfully however, Larry took it in stride and didn't slug me. I am still grateful today that he remained laid back in his demeanor and temperament. We finished our conversation, parted ways and again, I lost track of him.

About ten years passed. Once again, I was visiting my in-laws in Columbia, gravitating as I often did toward the Columbia Mall. And like déjà vu', it happened again: I ran into Larry. We were both happy to see each other. He didn't bring up the unpleasantness of our last encounter, although he did imply that it was a recollection. Nevertheless, he cheerfully informed me that his life was now focused on Christ. He said that soon after our last "providential" encounter many years before, he decided to return to his church. Years later, he was now a deacon in the church and happy to be serving in this leadership position (it was a Baptist church). He was happy and his family was happy. What a great memory! It is the last memory I have of Larry and it may be my final memory, because now, twenty plus years later, I do not remember his last name or know where he is.

CHRIST IS STILL CHANGING LIVES!

How much did I invest in Larry's life? The answer is clear: just a little in college, with the addition of two very brief encounters after college. The first encounter consisted of a little care and interest, along with some enthusiasm at seeing him once again. Then there was the curt comment, "Come on Larry, you can't let that happen!" That is about all I invested. Yet I was able to see God work in his life and raise him up for Christian leadership. I cannot really take credit for anything, except at least trying to speak into his life. God did the rest. And I was blessed with quite the memory and I share it with the reader. I often tell my students at RTS, "God is at work. He is doing things in people's lives. You can be assured of it! So, get involved, because you want to be present when God shows up! Nothing in life can top that!" So, I conclude by saying, "May you be a disciple investor in whatever way God leads you. And may you also watch him show up!"

Bibliography

Barna, George. *Growing True Disciples: New Strategies for Producing Genuine Followers of Christ.* Colorado Springs: Waterbrook, 2001.
Barna, George. *Revolution.* Carol Stream: Tyndale, 2005.
Bonhoeffer, Dietrich. *The Cost of Discipleship.* New York: Touchstone, 1995.
Clinton, Robert. *The Making of a Leader.* Colorado Springs: NavPress, 1988.
Coleman, Robert. *The Master Plan of Evangelism.* Grand Rapids: F.H. Revell, 1963.
Culbertson, Rod. *The "Disciple Investing" Life.* Eugene: Wipf and Stock, 2017.
Engle, James F., and Wilbert Norton. *What's Gone Wrong With the Harvest? A Communication Strategy for The Church and World Evangelism.* Grand Rapids: Zondervan, 1975.
Fillinger, Tom. "First Person–Measuring What Matters Most." *The Courier.* 2009. <http://baptistcourier.com/2009/05/first-person-measuring-what-matters-most/>.
Fryling, Alice. *Disciplemakers' Handbook: Helping People Grow in Christ.* Downers Grove: InterVarsity, 1989.
Griffiths, Michael. *God's Forgetful Pilgrims: Recalling the Church to Its Reason for Being.* 1975. Grand Rapids: Eerdmans, 1978.
Grubb, Norman, *C.T. Studd.* Fort Washington: Christian Literature Crusade, 1972.
Hadidian, Allen. *Successful Discipling.* Chicago: Moody, 1979.
Hendricks, Howard and William. *As Iron Sharpens Iron.* Chicago: Moody, 1995.
Henrichsen, Walter A. *Disciples Are Made–Not Born: Making Disciples Out of Christians.* Wheaton: Victor, 1974.
Hull, Bill. *The Complete Book of Discipleship: On Being and Making Followers of Christ.* Colorado Springs: NavPress, 2006.
———. *The Disciple Making Church.* Grand Rapids: F.H. Revell, 1990.
———. *The Disciple Making Pastor.* Grand Rapids: F.H. Revell, 1988.
International Consultation on Discipleship. *The Eastbourne Consultation Joint Statement on Discipleship.* Eastbourne, England. 1999.
Kuyper, Abraham. "Sphere Sovereignty." Free University. 1880. Public Address.
Lowrey, Mark. "The Primacy of Making Disciples - Whose Responsibility?" *Equip For Ministry,* 1999.
MacNair, Donald. *The Living Church: A Guide for Revitalization.* Philadelphia: Great Commission, 1980.

Metzger, Will. *Tell the Truth: The Whole Gospel to the Whole Person by Whole People*. 4th ed. Downers Grove: InterVarsity, 2012.

Miller, John. *Outgrowing the Ingrown Church*. Grand Rapids: Zondervan, 1986.

Miller, C. John. *Repentance and the 20th Century Man*. Fort Washington: Christian Literature Crusade, 1998.

Morley, Pat, David Delk, and Brett Clemmer. *No Man Left Behind: How to Build and Sustain a Thriving, Disciple-Making Ministry for Every Man in Your Church*. Chicago: Moody, 2006.

Murray, John. *Principles of Conduct: Aspects of Biblical Ethics*. 1957. Grand Rapids: Eerdmans, 1994.

Peterson, Eugene H. *A Long Obedience in the Same Direction: Discipleship in an Instant Society*. 2nd ed. Downers Grove: Intervarsity, 2000.

Pope, Randy. *The Journey: Maturing and Equipping Christ's Followers Through Life-on-life Missional Discipleship*. Duluth: Perimeter Church, 2007.

———. "What is Discipleship?" *Life on Life Journey Curriculum* from Perimeter Church. https://www.perimeter.org/pages/spiritual-growth/discipleship-2/the-journey-discipleship/.

Regele, Mike. *Death of the Church*. Grand Rapids: Zondervan, 1995.

RUF Staff Training Notebook.

Sinclair, David. *Biblical Discipleship*. Clemson, SC: Sinclair, 1991.

Stedman, Ray C. *Body Life: The Church Comes Alive*. Ventura: Regal, 1972.

Stott, John. "Make Disciples, Not Just Converts." *Christianity Today*. 1999. <http://www.christianitytoday.com/ct/1999/october25/9tc028.html>.

Tozer, A. W. *The Knowledge of the Holy*. New York: Harper & Brothers, 1961.

Wagner, C. Peter *Strategies for Church Growth*. Ventura: Regal, 1987.

———. *Your Church Can Grow*. Ventura: Regal, 1976.

Webber, Robert E. *Ancient-Future Evangelism*. Grand Rapids: Baker, 2003.

The Westminster Confession of Faith.

The Westminster Shorter Catechism.

www.ingramcontent.com/pod-product-compliance
Lightning Source LLC
Chambersburg PA
CBHW071509150426
43191CB00009B/1453